FOOD SAFETY
Law and Practice

AUSTRALIA
The Law Book Company
Brisbane - Sydney - Melbourne - Perth

CANADA
Carswell
Ottawa - Toronto - Calgary - Montreal - Vancouver

Agents
Steimatzky's Agency Ltd., Tel Aviv
N.M. Tripathi (Private) Ltd., Bombay
Eastern Law House (Private) Ltd., Calcutta
M.P.P. House, Bangalore
Universal Book Traders, Delhi
Aditya Books, Delhi
MacMillan Shuppan KK, Tokyo
Pakistan Law House, Karachi, Lahore

FOOD SAFETY
Law and Practice

by

CRAIG BAYLIS
Partner, Paisner & Co., Solicitors

with additional contributions by

DUNCAN MACLEOD
Barrister

and

KEVIN DEHAAN
Barrister

London
Sweet & Maxwell
1994

Published in 1994 by
Sweet & Maxwell Limited of
South Quay Plaza
183 Marsh Wall
London E14 9FT
Computerset by York House Typographic Ltd, London W13 8NT
Printed and bound in Great Britain by Hartnolls Ltd, Bodmin

No natural forests were destroyed to make this product;
only farmed timber was used and replanted

A CIP catalogue record for this book is
available from the British Library

ISBN 0-421-45760-0

Acknowledgments

The authors would wish to thank everyone involved in the production of the text, particularly Peter Glazebrook of Field Fisher Waterhouse for his original supervision of the text; Suzanne Davies for her contributions and forbearance in proof reading and to our colleagues in the food and drink industry. Without their expertise, advice and encouragement, this text could not have been produced.

Contents

Chapter 3
STATUTORY DEFENCES

Chapter 4
EMERGENCY PROHIBITION NOTICES AND ORDERS

Chapter 5
FOOD SAFETY LAW – THE EUROPEAN DIMENSION

Appendix
PART 1—FOOD SAFETY ACT 1990

PART 2—CODE OF PRACTICE NO. 6

Table of Cases

Table of Statutes

Table of Statutory Instruments

Table of European Cases

Table of European Materials

Introduction

The Law of Food Safety is a rigorously practical text. It is not an academic text book. The book deals with the practical application of recent legislation to food businesses. The book is a valuable guide and reference to all those concerned or participating in the food industry. Recent legislation relates to and affects directly all aspects of the supply, wholesale and retail food chain from production to consumption. Above all else the book is designed to render understandable the practical effects of recent legislation. The Food Safety Act 1990 is reproduced in the book for ease of reference. The text of the book explains and interprets the legislative framework and its effect. The book will provide a useful companion guide for proprietors, managers and employees within the food trade and industry and those who advise them, for persons working in county or district Food and Enforcement Authorities, for citizens advice bureaux and all people concerned with the legal aspects and enforcement of the law as it relates to food safety.

1

Some Useful Definitions

Throughout the Food Safety Act 1990 (hereafter referred to as the FSA), a number of words or phrases are constantly used which have a specific definition given to them for the purposes of the Act. It is important to bear in mind these extended definitions when considering any of the provisions of the FSA.

FOOD

Section 1 of the FSA defines "Food" to include:

(a) drink;
(b) items of no nutritional value which are used for human consumption *e.g.* bulking agents such as bran.
(c) chewing gum and similar products;
(d) anything used as an ingredient in the preparation of food.

Articles which are specifically excluded from the definition of "Food" include:

(a) live animals/birds or fish which are not used for human consumption while alive;
(b) animal feeds;
(c) controlled drugs (see Misuse of Drugs Act 1971);
(d) Medicines (see the Medicines Act 1968).

The supply of water is also specifically excluded from the definition by section 55 of the FSA. This is because the provisions of the Water Act 1989 (now the Water Resources Act 1991 and the Water Industry Act 1991) make specific provision for water suppliers and water undertakers to maintain certain standards in relation to water quality.

BUSINESS

Section 1(3) of the FSA defines a "Business" to include a canteen, club, school, hospital or institution whether carried on at a profit or not, and any similar activity carried on by a public or local authority.

FOOD BUSINESS

A Food Business is defined as any business (see above) in the course of which commercial operations with respect to food or food sources are carried out.

COMMERCIAL OPERATION

Commercial operation is defined as any of the following operations:

(a) selling, possessing for sale and offering/exposing/advertising for sale;
(b) consigning/delivering/serving by way of sale;
(c) preparing for sale or presenting/labelling/wrapping for sale;
(d) storing or transporting for sale;
(e) importing and exporting.

SALE

Section 2 of the FSA provides an extended definition of the ordinary meaning of the word "Sale" to include:

(a) the supply of food otherwise than on sale, in the course of a business; and
(b) any other thing which is done with respect to food and is specified in a Ministerial Order;

The supply of food otherwise than on sale in the course of a business would include situations where food is supplied at a subsidised rate, or free, to employees or clients provided that the supply is in the course of a business.

Section 2 also provides that the provisions of the FSA shall apply in relation to food which is offered as a prize or reward or given away in connection with any entertainment which is made available to the public.

4

Chapter 1

Control and Supervision of Food and Food Businesses

The Food Safety Act 1990 (the FSA) amends and builds on enforcement powers previously contained in the Food Act 1984 and incorporates new powers to enable Food Authorities to monitor and control the operation of food businesses.

THE ENFORCEMENT AUTHORITY   1–01

The relevant body for the purposes of the enforcement of legislation under the Food Safety Act is defined as the "Food Authority" in sections 5 and 6 of the FSA. In section 5(1)(a) the Food Authorities in England and Wales are defined as:

— the council of each London borough
— the relevant district council
— the relevant non-metropolitan county council
— the common council of the City of London
— the Treasurer of the Inner or Middle Temple

Because of the potential conflict in the exercise of functions under the Food Safety Act between "competing" Food Authorities, namely district councils and county councils, section 5(4) of the FSA provides that the relevant Minister may allocate specific functions under the FSA to either the district or the county councils. This power has been exercised through the Food Safety (Enforcement Authority England & Wales) Order 1990[1] to allocate the enforcement functions under section 12 of the FSA (Emergency Prohibition Notices and Orders) to local district councils.

The provisions of section 15 of the FSA (False Description/Presentation of Food) have likewise under the same Order been allocated to non-metropolitan county councils.

This allocation of responsibility is broadly in line with the present division of labour between the environmental health departments of district councils and the trading standards departments which are administered by county councils. The functions under section 15 of the FSA are certainly more akin to the field of trading standards and therefore more relevant to their existing functions.

1–02   Section 40 of the FSA gives power to the relevant Ministers to issue Codes of Practice for the guidance of Food Authorities. A number of these Codes of Practice have been issued, and Code of Practice No. 1 deals with the Responsibility for Enforcement of the Food Safety Act 1990. The importance of these Codes of Practice cannot be over-emphasised. The FSA creates an absolute duty under section 40(2) for every Food Authority to have regard to any relevant provision of any Code.

It becomes therefore most significant to be aware of the advice contained in any particular Code of Practice as such advice is bound to influence the manner in which food authorities perceive and carry out their duties under the Act.

In dealing with the division of responsibilities for enforcement between district and county councils the Code of Practice recognises the practical difficulties which may arise and therefore stresses the importance of close liaison arrangements between the authorities.

The Code advises in particular that:

> (a) If no liaison arrangements exist already, a co-ordinating group should be set up between the officers of the county and district councils, and where appropriate, the officers of the port health authority;
>
> (b) Co-ordinated advice on specific topics should be provided to businesses in the area;
>
> (c) Arrangements should be made for the transfer of complaints which have been received at the offices of one Food Authority but which are the responsibility of the other;

[1] S.I. 1990 No. 2462.

(d) Co-ordinated sampling programmes should be arranged;
(e) Recommendations on priorities for enforcement action should be adopted;
(f) Action should be co-ordinated on legal proceedings.

It is to be noted that *any* Food Authority may take legal proceedings under sections 7, 8 and 14 of the FSA. However, the Code of Practice on enforcement recommends division of responsibility as follows:

DISTRICT COUNCILS   1–03

1. Contamination of food by micro-organisms, *e.g.* salmonella, listeria, botulism;
2. Chemical contamination posing an *imminent risk to health*;
3. Contamination by mould or foreign matter, *e.g.* glass or metal shavings.

COUNTY COUNCILS

1. Chemical contamination and improper use of additives which *do not* pose an imminent risk to health;
2. Adulteration of food;
3. Misleading claims/advertisements;
4. Compositional problems associated with foods.

In any case where malicious tampering with food is suspected, the Food Authority should also involve the police in its investigations. The police may wish to consider potential offences of causing actual or grievous bodily harm in these circumstances, or the more specific offences of administering poison so as to endanger life or with intent to injure, under the Offences Against the Person Act 1861.

AUTHORISED OFFICERS   1–04

Authorised Officers of Food Authorities are defined in section 5(6) of the Food Safety Act 1990 as those persons authorised *in writing* by the Food Authority to act in matters arising under the FSA. In most circumstances, these officers will belong either to the environmental health department of a district council or the trading standards department of a county council.

1–05 Protection of Officers Acting in Good Faith

Immunity

Statutory immunity is provided to Authorised Officers of Food Authorities in their personal capacity by section 44 of the FSA. Similar legislation exists in relation to local authority officers exercising other functions.[2]

Section 44(1) of the FSA provides that the officer is not personally liable for acts done by him:

    (a) whilst executing or purporting to execute powers under the Act; and

    (b) whilst acting within the scope of his employment; and

    (c) that he acted in the honest belief that his duty under the Act required or entitled him to do so.

An officer of an authority for the purposes of this immunity will also include a public analyst appointed by a Food Authority.[3] It should be noted that the immunity granted by this section is in respect of *personal* liability only.

Section 42(2) of the FSA provides that the liability of the Food Authority in respect of the acts of its officers is not affected by the immunity granted by section 44(1).

1–06 *Indemnity*

Situations may arise where an officer of a Food Authority acts in the execution or purported execution of the Food Safety Act, but is, at the same time, acting outside the scope of his employment, *e.g.* in attempting to enforce provisions of the Act outside the geographical area of his employing authority.

In such circumstances, the authority is given a discretion by section 44(3) to indemnify him in respect of all or any part of damages or costs awarded against him, provided that the authority is satisfied that he honestly believed that the act complained of was within the scope of his employment.

As to the question of whether the belief of the officer is "honestly" held, see the two stage test applied in *R.* v. *Ghosh.*[4]

---

[2] See, *e.g.* Health and Safety at Work Act 1974, s. 26.
[3] FSA, s. 44(4).
[4] [1982] Q.B. 1053.

ENFORCEMENT POWERS

Power to Enter Premises (*section 32*)

When exercising their general powers to supervise food businesses, it is expected that most proprietors of those businesses will wish to provide voluntary assistance to enforcement agencies in order to maintain a friendly dialogue and an atmosphere of co-operation.

The Food Safety Act 1990, provides, however, for a specific power for Authorised Officers of enforcement agencies to enter premises, by force if necessary, in certain circumstances. This power is contained in section 32 of the FSA and largely repeats a similar provision which was contained in earlier legislation.[5]

The basic right to enter (section 32(1))

An authorised officer has a right to enter at all reasonable hours upon production (if so required) of a document showing his authority:

   (i) any premises within the authority's area for the purpose of ascertaining any contravention of the Food Safety Act 1990 or any associated regulations;

   (ii) any *business* premises either within or outside the authority's area in order to discover whether there is any evidence of any contravention within that area (this would also include movable or mobile premises);

   (iii) any premises for the performance of his functions under the Food Safety Act 1990, *e.g.* procuring samples, inspecting and seizing food likely to cause food poisoning.

N.B. Admission cannot be gained to a private dwelling house unless 24 hours notice of intention to enter is given to the occupier or the Authorised Officer is executing a warrant (see below).

---

[5] The Food Act 1984, ss. 87 and 88.

1-08 *Entry by warrant (section 32(2))*

In circumstances where entry to the premises is refused or is perceived as being likely to be refused, an Authorised Officer may apply to a Justice of the Peace on sworn information in writing for a warrant to enter premises if need be, by the use of reasonable force.

Before the warrant can be issued, the Justice of the Peace must be satisfied that there is a reasonable ground for entry (*e.g.* the exercise of a function under the FSA) *and* either:

(i) admission has been refused; or

(ii) admission is likely to be refused and notice of intention to apply for the warrant has been given to the occupier; or

(iii) application for admission, or the giving of such notice would defeat the object of entry (*e.g.* the occupier might take steps to dispose of evidence); or

(iv) the case is one of urgency; or

(v) the premises are unoccupied/the occupier is absent.

Warrants granted under this subsection remain in force only for a period of one month.

Under section 34(4) a specific duty is laid upon an Authorised Officer when leaving any unoccupied premises which have been entered by virtue of a warrant, to leave the premises as effectively secured as he found them. Failure to do so, and any subsequent loss from or damage to the premises, may render the officer executing the warrant, or the Food Authority employing the officer, liable in negligence.[6]

1-09 **Powers Upon Entry** (*section 32(5) & (6)*)

Any Authorised Officer entering premises under a warrant may take with him such other persons as he considers necessary, *e.g.* a police escort.

Whether entering under a warrant or under any other procedure, the officer has power to inspect any records including those held on computer, and may require any person concerned with the operation of the computer records to assist him in any reasonable way, *e.g.* by operation of the computer in order to produce intelligible data.

---

[6] However, see *ante*, Protection of officers acting in good faith (s. 44), para. 1–05 *et seq.*.

The officer is also empowered to *seize and detain* any records which might be required as evidence in subsequent proceedings, and to require records kept on computer to be produced in a form in which they may be taken away, *e.g.* print-outs of records held on computer disks.

This power to inspect, seize and detain records is a new power in the area of food safety law although it has for some time been available in other spheres of local authority supervision, *e.g.* the Health and Safety at Work, etc., Act 1974.

The power is likely to be exercised in circumstances where information is not provided voluntarily and may assist local authorities in ascertaining details of suppliers of food, dates of deliveries of suspect food or information required for the purposes of registration of a food business. (As to registration generally see section 19[7] and the relevant regulations.) In respect of other powers of inspection and seizure following entry to the premises see references to section 9 of the FSA.[8]

The Code of Practice dealing with powers of entry (Code of Practice No. 2–Legal Matters) clearly envisages that Authorised Officers may use their powers of entry to conduct extensive investigations once admission to the premises has been gained. Although there is no specific power in the FSA, the Code of Practice suggests that:

> "Authorised officers are empowered to inspect anything which may help establish whether or not an offence has been committed. This includes premises, equipment, machinery, food, processes . . . They may interview personnel and examine quality control systems . . . Officers may also take photographic and video evidence."

Given that there is no specific power of inspection except in relation to **1–10** records and suspect food[9] it must be assumed that the Code refers back to the general powers of an Authorised Officer to enter premises for the purpose of ascertaining whether any provision of the FSA has been contravened (section 32(1)(a)). This would include defective premises/ equipment which might be the subject of a Prohibition Order under section 11 of the FSA or an Improvement Notice under section 10 of the FSA. However, the exercise of these powers must always be subject to the general limitations imposed by virtue of the Police and Criminal Evidence Act 1984 and the Codes of Practice associated with that legislation.

---

[7] *post*, para. 1–49.
[8] *post*, para. 1–11.
[9] *Ibid.*

The admissibility of evidence in subsequent proceedings obtained in this manner would also be subject to the general rules of evidence which obtain in normal criminal trials, and in particular section 78 of the Police and Criminal Evidence Act 1984.

Unfortunately, the Code of Practice on dealing with powers of entry omits any reference to the need to administer a caution regarding self incrimination to persons who may be interviewed.

Such a reference is, however, specifically included in section 33(3) which deals primarily with the offence of obstruction of Authorised Officers.[10]

1–11 Powers to Inspect and Seize Suspected Food (*section 9*)

The power to inspect and seize food which may be unfit for human consumption is now contained in section 9 of the FSA. With some minor amendments, this section substantially reproduces and adds to a similar power which was available to Authorised Officers under sections 9 and 11 of the Food Act 1984.

The basic power under the Food Act 1984 merely allowed for seizure of suspect food by the Authorised Officer to enable him to apply to bring it before a Justice of the Peace in order to have it condemned and destroyed. The new power under section 9 of the FSA effectively divides into two parts; firstly a basic power to inspect food, and secondly a confiscation procedure for suspect food, exercisable initially by the Authorised Officer and thereafter to be confirmed by a Justice of the Peace in a procedure similar to that which was available for condemning food under section 9 of the Food Act 1984.

1–12 *The power to inspect (section 9(1))*

Section 9(1) of the FSA permits an Authorised Officer at *all reasonable times* to inspect any food intended for human consumption which either:

(a) has been sold, or is offered/exposed for sale; or
(b) is in the possession of or has been deposited with or consigned to any person for the purpose of sale or of preparation for sale.

---

[10] More specifically on this point, see *post*, para. 2–27 in relation to the offence of obstructing an Authorised Officer.

It is important to note that this power only arises in connection with food that is likely at some stage to be *sold* for human consumption. It need not necessarily refer to a *retail* sale and the power would therefore seem to extend to food which would be sold wholesale.

The power would *not* however seem to apply to food which is never intended for *sale* for human consumption, *e.g.* food which might be given away on a charitable basis. Reference must however always be made to the extended definition given to the meaning of "sale" in section 2 of the FSA. In that context, the word "sale" can also include a "supply" of food when carried out *in the course of a business*.

Note also the normal statutory presumption contained in section 3 of the FSA that any food which is commonly used for human consumption shall be presumed to have been intended for sale for human consumption until the contrary is proved. The power to inspect will also be exercisable following entry into premises by Authorised Officers either under section 32(1)(c)[11] or by virtue of a warrant issued under section 32(2).

It is interesting to note the use of the word "inspect" in this section **1–13** rather than the word "examine" which was used in the previously similarly-worded legislation under section 9 of the Food Act 1984. The Code of Practice issued to local authorities on inspection procedures[12] tends to suggest that the word "inspect" was chosen specifically to coincide with a range of enforcement procedures contained in the Control of Foodstuffs Directive.[13]

The Code of Practice envisages that an "inspection" of premises under section 9 of the FSA will have a quite specific and limited application. Such an inspection will involve a visit to food premises relating to a specific activity, *e.g.*:

— Inspection of premises
— Inspection of equipment
— Inspection of a process
— Inspection of hygiene practices
— Inspection of food
— Inspection of records
— Inspection of labels.

Certain types of visits to food premises are *not* regarded by the Code of Practice as an "inspection" for the purposes of section 9. These include:

---

[11] See *ante*, para. 1–07 for entry to premises for the purpose of performance of an authority's function under the FSA 1990.
[12] Code of Practice No. 3–Inspection Procedures—General.
[13] Directive 89/397.

— Visits solely to deal with complaints
— Visits solely to obtain samples
— Visits responding to requests for advice
— Visits to ensure compliance with an Enforcement Notice.

1–14   The Code of Practice envisages inspection taking place as part of a planned programme although as a general principle, the advice of the Control of Foodstuffs Directive[14] Article 4(4) is adopted; "Inspections shall be carried out without prior warning". This principle confirms the overriding aim of ensuring compliance with Food Safety legislation.

It is clear from the programmed inspection procedure that inspections are generally viewed as a procedure whereby operators of food businesses can be assisted and advised in their operations. This appears to be confirmed in the guidance on *post-inspection procedures* contained in the Code of Practice where Authorised Officers are advised to report back to the owner of the business following a programmed inspection. That report should include details of the inspection, the officer's conclusions and, in certain circumstances, should also set out action to be taken. This report may take the form of an Improvement Notice.[15]

More detailed Codes of Practice are available in relation to certain specific types of inspections; Code of Practice No. 8–Food Standards Inspections and Code of Practice No. 9–Food Hygiene Inspections. These Codes of Practice give valuable guidance and a remarkable insight into exactly how food authorities are advised to assess the risks of different types of food businesses in relation to their various operational procedures. More detailed consideration is given to these risk assessment inspection programmes below in relation to the "due diligence" defence, (see, *post*, Chapter 11).

1–15   *The confiscation/destruction procedure*

The confiscation procedure can arise in either of two circumstances:

1.   If an Authorised Officer finds upon an inspection under section 9(1), above, that any food fails to comply with food safety requirements (to ascertain whether food complies with food safety

---

[14] Directive 89/397, O.J. 1989. L186/23.
[15] As to Improvement Notices, see *post*, para. 1–22.

requirements, see section 8(2),[16] Selling Food not complying with Food Safety Requirements);

2. If it appears to an Authorised Officer *otherwise* than on an inspection under section 9 that food is likely to cause food poisoning or any disease communicable to human beings. This situation may arise where, for example, an Authorised Officer is acting on information received, possibly from a neighbouring Food Authority, without a previous inspection of the food.

The confiscation and subsequent destruction procedure in either case is exactly the same and allows an Authorised Officer to take one of two courses of action. He may either:

1. give Notice to the *person in charge of the food* (not necessarily the proprietor of the food business) that until the Notice is withdrawn, the food must not be used for human consumption and that the food must not be removed unless it is removed to some place specified in the Notice; or
2. seize the food and remove it in order to have it dealt with by a Justice of the Peace.

If the officer has proceeded by way of a Detention Notice (see 1 above) he **1–16** *must* as soon as reasonable practicable but in any event within 21 days, come to a decision as to whether or not the detained food complies with food safety requirements.

If he is so satisfied, the Notice should be withdrawn and the question of compensation considered.[17] If he is *not* so satisfied, the food must be removed to have it dealt with by a Justice of the Peace.

Although the Authorised Officer has 21 days in which to come to a decision as to whether or not food complies with food safety requirements, the Code of Practice in relation to inspection, detention and seizure of suspect food (Code of Practice No. 4) recommends a much shorter period. The Code states that "if possible the food should be dealt with by a Justice of the Peace within *two days*. In the case of highly perishable food, it should be dealt with by a Justice of the Peace as soon as possible".

Where officers have any doubts about suspect food being used for human consumption, it is recommended that the statutory procedures be adopted. It is important to note the statutory presumption that *all* food is intended for human consumption unless the contrary is proved (section 3(2) of the FSA).

---

[16] See *post*, para. 2–06.
[17] See *post*, para. 1–18.

1-17 *Disposal by a Justice of the Peace (section 9(6))*

The suspect food must at some stage be brought before a Justice of the Peace either through the Detention Notice procedure or directly following a seizure and removal of the suspect food.

Before the suspect food is dealt with by a Justice of the Peace, the officer exercising the power of seizure or detention must advise the person *in charge of the food* that it will be dealt with in that way. Any person who thereafter might be liable to prosecution under either sections 7 or 8 of the FSA (selling food not fit for human consumption or selling food not complying with food safety requirements) is entitled to appear before the Justice of the Peace and make representations and call witnesses if he chooses to do so.

Any Justice of the Peace who deals with the disposal of suspect food is not disqualified from sitting as a member of a Court which may subsequently deal with a prosecution under sections 7 or 8 of the FSA in relation to that food. However, it may be thought undesirable for the Justice of the Peace dealing with the disposal of the suspect food to participate in any subsequent criminal proceedings.

The Act is not very specific about the procedure to be adopted by the Justice of the Peace when considering the suspect food which is alleged to fail to comply with food safety requirements. Section 9(6) provides that a Justice of the Peace may condemn the food on the basis of "such evidence as he considers appropriate in the circumstances". This is a rather curious phrase which seems to allow for the Justice of the Peace, acting as an Examining Magistrate, to regulate his own proceedings although the rules of natural justice must inevitably apply to such proceedings.

This section compares to the previous corresponding section under the Food Act 1984 which simply provided that "if it appears to a Justice of the Peace that any food brought before him . . . ". There seemed to be no qualification to the previous power that the Justice of the Peace could consider such *evidence* as he thought "appropriate in the circumstances".

After hearing such evidence as he considers appropriate, if the Justice of the Peace considers that the food fails to comply with food safety requirements, he *must* condemn the food and also make two orders:

1. That the food be destroyed or disposed of to prevent it being used for human consumption; and
2. That the *owner* of the food should pay for all reasonable costs incurred in connection with the destruction or disposal of the food.

16

It should be noted that there is no provision within the Food Safety Act for any appeal against a decision of a Magistrate under section 9 to condemn the food, although, of course, such a decision would always be capable of judicial review in the High Court if the Magistrate had acted in excess of his powers, or had failed to take all relevant considerations into account.

Compensation   1–18

If the Justice of the Peace refuses to exercise his power under section 9 to condemn the food, *or* if a Detention Notice is withdrawn by the Food Authority before the suspect food is brought before a Justice of the Peace, then the Food Authority *must* compensate the owner of the food for any fall in its value which results in the action taken by the officer acting on behalf of the Food Authority.

Any dispute as to the amount of compensation to be paid or the right to compensation itself should be referred to arbitration. The Code of Practice on this matter urges the Food Authorities to agree at the time of seizure or detention any facts which would be relevant as to the question of the amount of compensation *e.g.*:

— The date of manufacture
— Shelf life
— Age of the food
— Quantity of the food
— Value of the food as paid for by the owner.

Either the Food Authority or the owner of the food concerned has the right to refer the matter to arbitration, and the arbitration itself will be governed by the Arbitration Acts.

Evidence of condemnation of suspect food in a   1–19
subsequent prosecution

It would not always be the case that a prosecution under section 7 or 8 of the FSA would automatically follow a condemnation order made by the Justice of the Peace.

There may be circumstances where the owner of the food might be completely blameless (*e.g.* where food in his possession had deliberately been tampered with in order to render it unfit for consumption).

In such circumstances, the Food Authority might agree to a voluntary procedure for disposal of the food. Food Authorities are warned, however, to give careful consideration to the use of such voluntary procedures in cases where a prosecution might subsequently result. This is because of the danger that a lack of formal seizure by way of a Detention Notice might be raised as part of a defence to such a prosecution, on the basis the food was not *so* contaminated that formal seizure had to take place. Such a suggestion could, of course, easily be rebutted either by scientific evidence as to the degree of contamination or evidence from the Authorised Officer that a voluntary procedure had been agreed with the owner of the suspect food as the most expeditious way of disposing of the food.

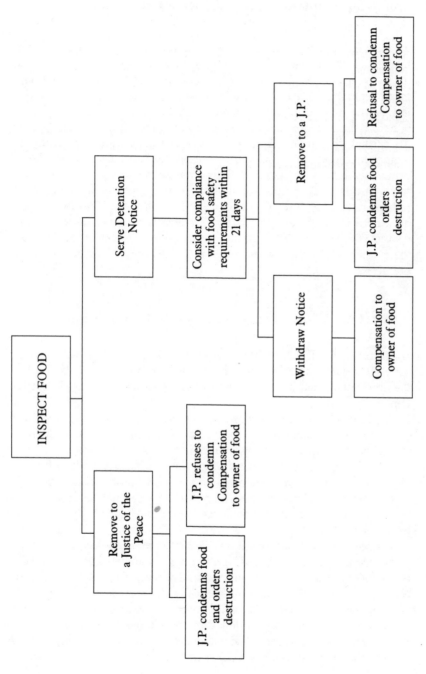

1–21 Improvement Notices (*section 10*)

The use of a system of enforceable notices requiring certain action to be taken is a new concept in Food Safety legislation. There was no corresponding provision in the Food Act 1984. However, the concept of statutory improvement notices is well known in other areas of legislation, particularly in the Health and Safety at Work, etc., Act 1974.

Before the implementation of section 10 of the FSA an informal procedure existed whereby the Authorised Officer of the Enforcement Authority might request, either verbally or in writing, that certain action be taken to bring premises up to standard. There was, however, very little effective sanction that could be brought to bear if the proprietor of the premises refused to comply with such a request. The only other possibility might have been to institute a prosecution for breach of any of the regulations dealing with hygiene or processing. Even in those circumstances, however, there would still be no power to require that work be carried out on the premises.

1–22 *The Basic Power under section 10 of the FSA.*

An Authorised Officer has power to serve an Improvement Notice on the proprietor of a food business if he has reasonable grounds for believing that the proprietor is failing to comply with any regulations to which the section applies.

The Improvement Notice must be signed *only* by officers authorised to do so by an Enforcement Authority. Such officers will include Environmental Health Officers with experience in food law enforcement.

The original Code of Practice on Improvement Notices (Code of Practice No. 5—The Use of Improvement Notices) was revised and re-issued in April 1994 to clarify some areas of practice by Enforcement Authorities which had been the subject of debate when the original Code was first issued in 1990.

It is now clearly established in the Code that where Officers who are not authorised to sign Improvement Notices carry out an inspection, an Authorised Officer should also have witnessed a contravention which justifies the Notice, so that the Authorised Officer can sign and issue the Notice.

There has clearly been some anxiety about the fact that Officers without relevant experience have been allowed by some authorities to issue Notices. Authorities are therefore reminded in the Code that inappropriate or wrongful service of a Notice can result in a Court award for costs against the Authority.

In *Nakuda Ali* v. *M.F. de S. Jayaratne,*.[18] a similar question arose in relation to regulations which allowed the Controller of Textiles in Ceylon to cancel a Textile Licence which had been issued under the relevant regulations where "the Controller has reasonable grounds to believe" that any dealer is unfit to be allowed to continue as a dealer. In the House of Lords, it was decided that those words were to be treated as imposing a condition that there must, in fact, exist such reasonable grounds, *known to the Controller*, before he could validly exercise the power of cancellation.

The relevant regulations 1–23

The power arises in relation to any regulations which make provisions:

(a) For requiring, prohibiting or regulating the use of any process or treatment in the preparation of food; or
(b) For securing the observance of hygienic conditions and practices in connection with the carrying out of commercial operations with respect to food or food sources.

In practice, this means any regulations dealing with food hygiene or food processing.[19]

The contents of the Notice 1–24

When the Notice is served on the proprietor of the food business it should:

(a) State the officer's grounds for believing that the proprietor is failing to comply with the relevant regulations;
(b) Specify the matters which constitute the failure to comply;
(c) Specify the measures which the proprietor must take to secure compliance;
(d) Require the proprietor to take those measures within a specific period (not being less than 14 days from the date of the notice).

A statutory instrument, The Food Safety (Improvement and Prohibition—Prescribed Forms) Regulations 1991[20] has been issued to provide for

---

[18] [1951] A.C. 66.
[19] See Code of Practice No. 6, Schedule of Hygiene and Processing Regulations, reproduced at p. 169.
[20] S.I. 1991 No. 100.

a standard form which may be used for Authorised Officers in serving Improvement Notices.

In *London Borough of Bexley* v. *Gardner Merchant Plc*, (unreported), in a judgment given by the Divisional Court of the Queen's Bench Division on March 17, 1993, Lord Justice Evans confirmed that the Notice under section 10 must specify what it is that the person to whom the Notice is addressed, has failed to do. The Notice must be specific, and not simply recite the Food Hygiene Regulations which have been contravened, but must deal in detail with exactly what is required to remedy the defects with which the Notice is concerned. The revised Code of Practice confirms this advice from the Court of Appeal.

The judgment also confirmed that it is not possible for the Magistrates' Court to put right any defects in the Notice by virtue of their power to vary the Notice on appeal under section 39 of the FSA.

1–25 *The Offence*

It is an offence to fail to comply with an Improvement Notice punishable either in the Magistrate's Court or in the Crown Court. In the Magistrate's Court, the maximum fine is one not exceeding Level 5 on the standard scale (at present £5,000) or to imprisonment for a term not greater than six months, or both. In the Crown Court upon conviction, an unlimited fine may be imposed or a term of imprisonment not greater than two years, or both.

1–26 *Appeals*

Section 37 (1) of the FSA provides that any person who is aggrieved by a decision of an Authorised Officer to serve an Improvement Notice may appeal to a Magistrate's Court.

In theory at least, the right of appeal is not limited simply to the person upon whom the notice is served (the proprietor of the food business), but may also extend to any person aggrieved by the decision to serve the notice. This might include the manager of the business, or members of staff who may be affected by any measures which have to be taken to comply with the notice.

Section 39 of the FSA deals specifically with the Court's powers on the hearing of the appeal at which time the Court may either cancel or affirm the notice. If the court affirms the notice it may do so either in its original form, or by varying the terms of the notice in such manner as the Court thinks fit.[21] Lodging of an appeal automatically suspends the period of compliance with the Notice until such time as the appeal has been determined.[22] There is a further right of appeal to the Crown Court if the Magistrates dismiss the appeal.[23]

The revised Code of Practice seems to have taken account of criticisms of the original Code and the inconsistent use of Improvement Notices by different Enforcement Authorities.

The revised Code now makes it clear that it is still perfectly acceptable and indeed desirable in the first instance, to adopt informal procedures to secure compliance with food hygiene regulations within a reasonable time. Such informal procedures could include a letter of advice indicating the recommendations of the Authorised Officer.

Guidance is given as to the circumstances when it might be appropriate to issue an Improvement Notice:

(a) where formal action is proportionate to the risk to health;
(b) where there is a previous history of failure to comply with food safety legislation;
(c) where the Authorised Officer has reason to believe that an informal approach will be unsuccessful.

Authorised Officers are reminded that when conditions pose an imminent risk to health, then action under section 12 (Emergency Prohibition Notices and Orders[24]) may be the more appropriate course of action to pursue.

There are certain circumstances where it would clearly be inappropriate to issue a Notice:

(a) where the contravention does not pose a serious or imminent risk to health, e.g. minor decorative faults in food preparation areas;
(b) in situations of limited duration, e.g. a one day festival or sporting event.

It is emphasised that the issue of a Notice does not prevent the Enforcement Authority from pursuing a subsequent prosecution for breaches of Regulations which were the subject of a Notice. Indeed, the Enforcement Authority might be open to criticism if it failed to ensure that inappropriate conditions were not remedied as soon as possible.

---

[21] FSA 1990, s. 39(1).
[22] Ibid., s. 39(2).
[23] Ibid., s. 38(9).
[24] See post, para. 1–37.

1–28 Prohibition Orders (*section 11*)

Introduction and scope of the Order

Section 11 of the FSA introduces a new system of control of food premises by means of the Prohibition Order.

The Prohibition Order is a Court Order which must be issued when certain criteria are established following a conviction in court. The effects of the Order may be extensive, even as far as closing down the food business, until the local Food Authority is satisfied that the circumstances which gave rise to the Order have been put right. The Order effectively becomes part of the sentencing process of the court.

1–29 *Circumstances for making the Order*

By section 11(1) of the Act, the Order *must* be imposed by a court if:

(a) the proprietor of a food business is convicted of an offence under the regulations to which the section applies; and

(b) the court is satisfied that the "health risk condition" is fulfilled.

The Code of Practice on prohibition procedures[25] confirms that the relevant regulations for the purposes of (a) above are those concerned with hygiene or food processing. A list of the relevant regulations is set out in the schedule to the Code of Practice,[26] but the most important for all practical purposes are the Food Hygiene (General) Regulations 1970.[27]

1–30 *When is the "health risk" condition fulfilled?*

Section 11(2) of the FSA defines the health risk condition as being fulfilled if any of the following involves "risk of injury to health":

(a) the use of any process or treatment for the purposes of the business;

(b) the construction of any premises or the use of any premises for the purposes of the business;

---

[25] Code of Practice No. 6.
[26] See Code of Practice No. 6, Schedule of Hygiene and Processing Regulations, reproduced at p. 169.
[27] S.I. 1970 No. 1172, as amended by S.I. 1990 No. 1431.

(c) the state or condition of any premises or equipment used for the purposes of the business.

There is no qualification in the Act as to the use of the words "risk of injury to health." There is certainly no requirement for the purposes of *this* section that the risk be imminent or of a certain category or magnitude. It would seem that any risk, however remote or trivial, would be adequate to fulfil the health risk and condition provided that it gave rise to a "risk of injury to health." The relevant Code of Practice sheds little further light on the interpretation of this phrase, although there is considerable discussion of the phrase in relation to the exercise of Food Authority powers to issue a Prohibition *Notice* under section 12.[28]

The effect of the Order

1–31

If there is a conviction under the relevant regulations and the court considers that the health risk condition is fulfilled, it *must* make one of the following orders:

1. Prohibit the use of the process or treatment in a case falling within (a) above;
2. Prohibit the use of the premises or equipment in a case falling within (b) above;
3. Prohibit the use of the premises or equipment in a case falling within (c) above for the purposes of *any* food business.[29]

Additionally, the court may impose a Prohibition Order on the *proprietor* to prevent him from participating in the management of a food business if:

1. he is convicted of an offence involving food hygiene practices; and
2. the court thinks it proper to do so.

In theory at least, this power could apply equally to corporate proprietors of food businesses as well as individuals, and could have significant effect on companies which operate a number of food businesses either locally or nationally.[30]

It is submitted that a court would have to have substantial evidence from which it could order a prohibition on any particular *class* of food business where the effect of such an order would be to close more than one particular

1–32

---

[28] See *post*, para. 1–37.
[29] FSA 1990, s. 11(3).
[30] *Ibid.*, s. 11(4).

set of business premises. Such evidence would have to amount to a significant flaw in the proprietor company's methods of business in all of their food operations, and not merely a negligent dereliction of duty in one particular set of premises.

This power applies equally to the manager of a food business as it does to the proprietor of such a business.[31] The term "manager" is specifically defined by section 11(11) of the FSA, as any person who is entrusted by the proprietor with the day to day running of the business, or any part of the business. This definition seems to envisage that the proprietor will have taken specific steps to delegate the daily control of the business or part thereof to another person.

1–33 *The role of the Food Authority*

Immediately following the making of the Order under section 11, the Food Authority is entrusted with the role of supervising the Order.

Following the making of the Order itself by the court under the terms either of section 11(3) or 11(4), the Food Authority must:

1. serve a copy of the Order on the proprietor of the business; and
2. in the case of an Order under section 11(3) relating to specific premises, the authority must affix a copy of the Order in a conspicuous position to those premises.

1–34 *Lifting the Order*

An Order under section 11(3) which relates to the use of a process/premises/ equipment can be lifted by the Enforcement Authority by way of a Certificate of Satisfaction. An Order under section 11(4) relating to a prohibition on a proprietor or a manager can be lifted *only by the Court*.

Prohibition on the Use of a Process/Premises/Equipment (*section 11(3)*)

— Section 11(6) (a) provides that the Order shall cease to have effect when the Enforcement Authority issues a Certificate of Satisfaction that the proprietor has taken enough measures to ensure that the health risk condition is no longer fulfilled.

---

[31] *Ibid.*, s. 11(10).

— The Proprietor may apply to the Food Authority for the grant of such a Certificate and the Food Authority *must* determine the application within 14 days of receipt.
— The Authority *must* issue the Certificate within three days of being so satisfied.
— If the Food Authority is not so satisfied following an application by a proprietor, then a Notice must be served on the proprietor giving reasons for that decision.

Prohibition Order on a Proprietor or Manager (*section 11(4)*) 1–35

— This Order can *only* be lifted by a direction by the court to that effect (section 11(6)(b))
— The Proprietor or manager who is the subject of the Order may make an application to the Court to have the Order lifted, but not before:

1. Six months have elapsed since the making of the Order; nor
2. Within three months after the making of a previous application for such a direction by a proprietor or manager.[32]

The net effect of these provisions is to ensure that a Court Order cannot be imposed for a shorter period than six months, as there is no guidance laid down in the Act as to whether the initial order may be circumscribed by any conditions or time limits.

Appeals 1–36

All of the Prohibition Order procedures are subject to review. Section 37 of the FSA provides for a right of appeal to the Magistrate Court against a decision of a Food Authority to refuse to issue a certificate under section 11(6)(a) that the health risk condition is no longer fulfilled.[33] Section 38 of the FSA contains a right of appeal to the Crown Court against the decision of a Magistrate's Court to issue a Prohibition Order.

The right of appeal in each case is available to "any person who is aggrieved" by the relevant decision. In practice, this could extend to any person who may be affected by the decision, and need not simply be the

---

[32] FSA 1990, s. 11(8).
[33] See *ante*, para. 1–34.

proprietor of the food business, *e.g.* members of staff whose jobs depend on the local business.

In the case of an appeal under section 37, the appeal must be brought within one month from the date on which notice of the decision was served.[34]

In respect of an appeal under section 38 to the Crown Court, the normal time limit of not more than 21 days after the day on which the decision appealed against is given will apply. This time limit can be found in rules 6 and 7 of the Crown Court Rules 1982.

No guidance is obtained either from the Acts or the Codes of Practice on when it might be appropriate to pursue an appeal. However, at least as far as the refusal by a Food Authority to issue a certificate under section 11(6)(a) is concerned, reasons for the refusal must be given under section 11(7)(b). It may therefore be fairly easy to determine whether the reasons given in such a case might provide for an appeal; for example, if the reasons given for the decision appear to be based on irrelevant considerations.

1–37 Emergency Prohibition Notices and Orders

Emergency Prohibition Notice—Introduction

The system of Emergency Prohibition Notices is a completely new enforcement measure introduced by the FSA. This procedure can enable the local Food Authority to take drastic action in respect of food business premises where it is believed that very rapid action is required. The relevant Code of Practice provides examples of situations where an Emergency Prohibition Notice might be appropriate: serious infestation of premises by vermin leading to a real risk of food contamination, use of defective equipment such as a refrigerator incapable of achieving the appropriate operating temperatures or a process involving a serious risk of cross-contamination.

The procedures under section 11 of the FSA for application to the Court for a Prohibition Order can only apply following conviction of the proprietor of a food business for breach of regulations. The procedure under section 12 of the FSA for an Emergency Prohibition Notice can enable a Food Authority to shut down a food business with immediate effect, and without any prior warning, although the Food Authority must be prepared to justify its actions before the Magistrates Court in due course.

---

[34] See FSA 1990, s. 37(5)(a).

Circumstances for serving the Emergency Prohibition Notice

1–38

The Notice can be served when an Authorised Officer of an Enforcement Authority is satisfied that the health risk condition is fulfilled (section 12(1)). Contrast the requirements in this sub-section with that contained in section 10(1) in relation to Improvement Notices—"if an Authorised Officer of an Enforcement Authority has reasonable grounds for believing . . ."

Again the Code of Practice offers little guidance on the question of whether the Authorised Officer must be personally satisfied that the health risk condition is fulfilled, although the case of *Nakuda Ali* v. *M.F. de S Jayaratne* (see *ante*) would nevertheless be relevant.

The definition of "health risk condition" for these purposes is the same as that used for the purposes of consideration of a Prohibition Order under section 11.[35]

It must *also* be shown however that the risk of injury to health is an *imminent risk* (section 12(4)).

The words "imminent risk" are not specifically defined in the FSA, but helpful guidance as to what might constitute an imminent risk are given in the Code of Practice on prohibition procedures.[36]

Voluntary Procedures

1–39

Although the Code of Practice envisages that an Emergency Prohibition Notice will be served in almost every circumstance where an imminent risk of injury to health exists, there are possible advantages to the Food Authority in pursuing a voluntary offer by the proprietor to close his premises. This is because section 12(10) provides for a mandatory compensation procedure to the owner of the food business where an Emergency Prohibition Notice is served and the Magistrate's Court subsequently finds that there were no preconditions to justify the service of the notice. Clearly, therefore, if the voluntary procedure is adopted, no notice is served and the mandatory compensation provisions cannot operate.

---

[35] See subs. 11(2) and (3).
[36] See Introduction above.

It is interesting to compare these recommendations on the use of voluntary procedures with those which are recommended in the Code of Practice relating to inspection, detention and seizure of suspect food.[37]

The Code of Practice in relation to Emergency Prohibition Notices requires that where the proprietor offers to close voluntarily, it must be made quite clear that if he chooses to do so, he will relinquish any rights to compensation which would have existed under section 12(10).

1–40 *Procedure for service of the Notice*

Section 12(1) requires that the Emergency Prohibition Notice be served on the proprietor of the business. Section 50 of the FSA deals with service of documents and section 50(2) provides that the Notice may be delivered to some person on the premises or affixed to some conspicuous part of the premises if the premises are unoccupied or it is not practicable to ascertain the name and address of the person on whom it should be served.

Service by hand or at a company's registered office either by hand or by post or at a person's usual or last known address by hand or post will constitute good service of the Notice. It should be remembered that a company's registered office in the case of national or multi-national corporations may be many hundreds of miles distant from the operation which is to be closed down. The Code of Practice requires that every effort should be made to serve the Notice on the proprietor by hand.

In the case of a business operated as a partnership every effort should be made to serve each and every one of the partners of the business although the Notice is legally served as soon as it is properly served on any one of the partners.

Section 12(5) of the FSA requires that the Enforcing Authority should also fix a copy of the Notice to the relevant premises as soon as practicable after service of the Notice.

1–41 *Procedure following service of the Notice*

It should be appreciated that the Emergency Prohibition Notice procedure is regarded by FSA as a purely temporary arrangement until such time as the prohibition contained in the Notice can be ratified (if appropriate) by the Magistrates Court in the form of an Emergency Prohibition *Order*.

---

[37] See *ante*, para. 1–11.

The Enforcing Authority is therefore required to apply to the Magistrates Court for an Emergency Prohibition *Order* within three days of the service of the Emergency Prohibition *Notice*.

Failure to make the application within the appropriate time limit will result in the Emergency Prohibition Notice ceasing to have effect[38] and also rendering the Enforcing Authority potentially liable to pay compensation to the proprietor of the business—(section 12(10)(a)).

The three day time limit in respect of which an application must be made   **1–42** is calculated by reference to the date upon which the application papers are submitted to the Magistrates Court. In *Farrand* v. *Tse*[39] the Authorised Officer lodged the relevant application papers for an Order under section 12(2) of the FSA within three days of service of a notice under section 12(1) of the FSA. The Magistrates did not hear the application until after the three days. Following a submission, the Magistrates decided that the date the application was made is the date of the hearing, and they thereupon dismissed the application. The Enforcing Authority appealed to the High Court which decided that the Magistrates had been wrong in their decision because the application was *made* when the papers were lodged with the Magistrates Court.

The Authorised Officer of the Enforcement Authority must also at least one day before the date of the application for the Emergency Prohibition Order, serve notice of his intention so to apply upon the proprietor of the business concerned.[40] The provisions of section 50 of the FSA[41] will once more apply to service of this Notice.

Provided that the application for the Emergency Prohibition Order is made within three days of service of the Emergency Prohibition Notice, the Notice will remain in force until such time as the Magistrates Court has been able to determine the application for the Order, or the application is withdrawn.[42]

The Emergency Prohibition Order   **1–43**

Although some limited guidance is given to the Court as to the circumstances in which a Prohibition Order should be made under section 11 (*i.e.*
if the Court thinks it proper to do so in all the circumstances, section

---

[38] See s. 12(7)(a).
[39] *The Times*, December 10, 1992, D.C.
[40] See s. 12(3).
[41] See *ante*, para. 1–40.
[42] See s. 12(7)(b).

11(4)(b)) better guidance is available from the FSA in relation to Emergency Prohibition Orders made under section 12(2). By virtue of that subsection, the Court *must* impose the appropriate prohibition if it is satisfied that the "health risk condition" is fulfilled with respect to that food business. For the purposes of section 12, the criteria for fulfilment of the 'health risk condition' are exactly the same as those set out in section 11(2).[43]

These *should* be the same criteria as those applied by the Authorised Officer in the case who would have been responsible for taking the initial decision to issue the Emergency Prohibition Notice.

The Code of Practice advises the Authorised Officer to continue to monitor the affected premises following service of the Emergency Prohibition Notice until the Court hearing for the Emergency Prohibition Order. This is to enable the Authorised Officer to continue to gather evidence to put before the Court on the hearing of the Emergency Prohibition Order, as the state of the premises may have changed, or other circumstances may have arisen which give rise to a further risk to health.

The Code of Practice requires that the Authorised Officer should take detailed contemporaneous notes during his inspection in relation to the matters which give rise to service of the Emergency Prohibition Notice. Evidence may include sketches, photographs and samples.

The Order which may be imposed by the court shall be in respect of the appropriate prohibition. For the purposes of section 12(2) of the FSA, the appropriate prohibition is the same as those contained in section 11(3).[44]

There is however no provision in respect of the *Emergency* Notice Order procedure for the prohibition of a *Proprietor* participating in the management of a food business. Contrast this with the provisions of section 11(4) of the FSA which enable a Court to apply such a prohibition in particular circumstances.[45]

Although no specific procedure is set out in the FSA for hearing of the Emergency Prohibition Order, it is submitted that as the application is one for an Order, the usual Magistrates Courts Act 1980 procedure for dealing with an Order by way of Complaint should be followed.

The procedure in such circumstances is set out in section 53 of the Magistrates Courts Act 1980 and section 53(2), provides for both sides to be heard in that: "The Court, after hearing the evidence and the parties shall

---

[43] See *ante*, paras. 1–30 and 1–38.
[44] See *ante*, 1–31—the Effect of the Order.
[45] *Ibid.*

make the Order for which the Complaint is made or dismiss the Complaint."

In these circumstances, the position as to costs is governed by section 64 of the Magistrates' Courts Act 1980 so that either party may recover costs of the legal proceedings against the other if successful.

Lifting the Notice/Order 1–44

The Notice

The Emergency Prohibition Notice can cease to have effect in three ways:

1. If no application for Emergency Prohibition Order is made within three days of service of Emergency Prohibition Notice, at the end of that three day period[46]; or
2. Upon the determination of such an application by the Court[47]; or
3. By the issue of a Certificate of Satisfaction by the Enforcing Authority.[48]

The Order

The Emergency Prohibition Order may only be lifted by a Certificate of Satisfaction under section 12(8).

The Certificate of Satisfaction 1–45

Applications for the Certificate of Satisfaction may be made by the Proprietor of the food business concerned. The criteria for the issue of the Certificate which are laid down in section 12(8) are simply that the Food Authority should be satisfied that the Proprietor has taken sufficient measures to secure that the health risk condition is no longer fulfilled.

The application for the Certificate which is made by the Proprietor of the food business should be made in writing. Section 49(1)(b) requires that all applications required under the Act to be given or made to any officer of a Food Authority shall be in writing. This might be thought to be unduly harsh in circumstances where it may be essential to re-open the business quickly, and the making of an application in writing (*e.g.* over a weekend or

---

[46] s. 12(7)(a).
[47] See s. 12(7)(b).
[48] See s. 12(8).

33

during a period when the Food Authority offices are closed) would not be possible.

There does however seem to be no bar in the FSA to the Food Authority issuing the necessary certificate of its own volition, if it appears to the Authority on a subsequent inspection, that the proprietor has fulfilled the criteria set out in section 12(8) of the FSA. This is a course of action which does not appear to be contemplated by the Code of Practice, although it would not appear to be excluded by the statutory provisions.

The question as to whether the Certificate can be issued must be determined by the Authority as soon as reasonably practicable and at the latest within 14 days of the application for the Certificate.[49]

The Code of Practice confirms that the premises should be revisited as soon as possible.

If the Authority is satisfied that the Certificate can be issued it must do so as quickly as possible or at the latest within three days of that determination.

The Code of Practice makes it clear that the Certificates can be issued by fax and also contemplates that the Authority should allow the Proprietor to re-open the premises immediately.

If the Authority is not satisfied that the relevant criteria under section 12(8) have been fulfilled, then a notice of continuing risk to health should be issued to the Proprietor, and reasons given for that determination.

1–46 *Official removal of Notices or Orders*

It will be remembered that the provisions of subsections (5) and (6) of section 12 of the FSA require that the Enforcement Authority must affix a copy of the Notice or Order in a conspicuous position on the premises which are affected.

The unauthorised removal or defacement of such a Notice or Order would certainly be an offence under section 1 of the Criminal Damage Act 1971, although there is no specific provision in the FSA to create a separate offence of unauthorised removal or defacement of Statutory Notices or Orders.

The Code of Practice reminds Authorised Officers that section 63 of the Magistrates Court Act 1980 enables a court making an Order to make provisions ancillary to it. It is suggested therefore that the Authorised Officer should request the court making the Emergency Prohibition Order

---

[49] s. 12(9)(a).

to attach a condition that the Order should not be defaced or removed by any unauthorised person.

An Offence under section 63 of the Magistrates Courts Act 1980 could of course only apply to an unauthorised removal of defacement of an Order made by a court. It could not apply to an Emergency Prohibition Notice which has been issued by an Enforcing Authority.

The penalty for breach of a condition attached to an Order under section 63 of the Magistrates Courts Act 1980, is a maximum fine of £5,000 or imprisonment of a term not exceeding two months or a fine of £50 for every day during which a breach of the condition continues.

Compensation 1–47

Section 12(10) imposes a positive duty upon an Enforcement Authority to compensate the Proprietor of a food business for any losses suffered by reason of compliance of an Emergency Prohibition Notice. The only way in which the enforcing authority can avoid this duty is to ensure:

1. That an application for an Emergency Prohibition Order is made within three days of service of the Emergency Prohibition Notice[50]; and
2. On the hearing of the application for the Emergency Prohibition Order, the Court is satisfied that the health risk condition was fulfilled at the time that the Emergency Prohibition Notice was served.

Any dispute in respect of the amount of compensation payable should be determined by arbitration.

The Code of Practice provides assistance as to the matters which may be taken into account when assessing the amount of compensation to be paid. This list is not exhaustive and deals with such matters as:

— The length of the prohibition period;
— Loss of trade;
— Value of spoiled food;
— Loss of good will;
— Loss of wages;
— Amount of damage made which is recoverable;
— The duty of the proprietor to mitigate his loss.

---

[50] See s. 12(7)(a).

It is recommended that a Loss Adjuster may be called in if both parties agree. In cases of disagreement, the Food Authority should seek to resolve the dispute informally by meeting and discussion with the Proprietor. Arbitration is to be viewed very much as a last resort.

1–48 *Appeals*

No form of statutory appeal lies against the decision of an Enforcement Officer to issue an Emergency Prohibition Notice. That decision is, however, inherently reviewable because of the requirement to apply within three days of service of the Emergency Prohibition Notice to the Magistrates Court for an Emergency Prohibition Order. An appeal lies to the Crown Court from a decision of the Magistrates Court to issue an Emergency Prohibition Order under section 38(b) of the FSA. Such an appeal may be pursued by any person who is aggrieved by the decision of the Magistrates Court to make the Order.

The term "any person who is aggrieved" is not defined in the FSA and may include not only the Proprietor of the business, but also any other person affected by the decision such as an employee of the food business, or even a supplier of the business. The Enforcement Authority has no right of appeal to the Crown Court in a situation where the Magistrates Court refuses to issue an Emergency Prohibition Order.

1–49 REGISTRATION AND LICENSING OF FOOD BUSINESS PREMISES

Introduction

When the Bill which was eventually to become the Food Safety Act 1990 was being considered, it was suggested that there might be much good sense in creating a system of registration and licensing of food business premises to more efficiently monitor and control food operations in their areas. These ideas eventually found form in section 19 of the FSA.

The proposals in respect of the licensing of food premises were felt however to be so far reaching in terms of the potential economic impact on food business operators, that a provision was inserted into section 19 to ensure that the licensing of food businesses would be introduced only in

36

certain circumstances.[51] To date, no system of licensing has been introduced.

The registration provisions are now in force. The rationale behind the registration of food business premises is set out in the relevant Code of Practice:

> "the purpose of registration is to provide information to food authorities responsible for enforcing food law about food businesses in their area, so that they can target their enforcement resources more effectively. It is intended that food authorities should use the information provided by registration to help plan their inspection programmes."

Registration of Food Businesses   1–50

The power to require registration is contained in simple terms in section 19(1)(a) of the Food Safety Act, in a "framework" section which allows the Ministers to make regulations for the registration of food business premises and prohibit the use of such premises which are not so registered.

The relevant regulations the Food Premises (Registration) Regulations 1991[52] came completely into force on July 1, 1992 although the main provisions of the regulations involving the basic requirement to register came into force on May 1, 1991.

The Registration Authority   1–51

The authority to whom applications should be made for registration is also the Enforcement Authority as defined in regulation 9 of the Regulations. This means the district councils in England and Wales or the relevant London borough in the London area. Where the functions of the Food Authority are assigned to a Port Health or Port Local Authority, then that authority also becomes a Registration Authority.

---

[51] See *post*, para. 1–50.
[52] S.I. 1991 No. 2825.

1-52 *The Duty to Register*

Instead of imposing a positive duty to register certain premises upon the relevant persons, the regulations chose to impose a prohibition on the use of premises unless they have been registered. It must therefore first be ascertained exactly when there arises a need to register premises.

That need arises where premises are used for the purposes of a food business on *five or more days* (whether consecutive or not) *in any period of five consecutive weeks*, unless the premises are exempt from registration.[53]

What are "Premises"

"Premises" are not defined in the regulations. Definitions are however provided for "permanent premises" and "moveable premises". These are two definitions which seem to be mutually exclusive and which therefore taken together can be said effectively to define the use of the word "premises" *in toto*.

— *Permanent premises* are defined as land or buildings.
— *Moveable premises* are defined as premises other than permanent premises, and "relevant moveable premises" means moveable premises used for the transport or preparation of food or retail sale of food on five or more days (whether consecutive or not) in any period of five consecutive weeks. This would include such vehicles as hot dog stalls, and ice cream vans which are used for relevant period of time. Moveable premises *per se* are *exempt* from registration but their use may give rise to register permanent premises if moveable premises are kept there.

Are the Premises Used for the Purposes of a Food Business?

— A *food business* is defined not in the Regulations, but in section 1(3) of the FSA itself as "any business in the course of which *commercial operations* with respect to food or food sources are carried out".
— A *commercial operation* in relation to food in specifically defined also in section 1(3) of the FSA as any of the following:

    (i) selling/possessing for sale and offering, exposing or offering for sale;
    (ii) consigning, delivering or serving by way of sale;

---

[53] As to exemptions see *post*, para. 1–57.

(iii) preparing for sale or presenting labelling or wrapping for the purpose of sale;

(iv) storing or transporting for the purpose of sale;

(v) importing and exporting—in deciding whether or not a commercial operation is being carried out it is essential to remember that section 2(1) of the FSA extends the definition of "sale" to include the *supply* otherwise than on sale, in the course of a business.

— This extension of the definition therefore includes operations such as factory or office facilities where food might be provided free of charge to employees or clients on a regular basis within the five day rule.[54]

Moveable Premises

1–54

In most circumstances, moveable premises *per se* are exempt from registration. The phrase moveable premises includes tents, marquees and awnings, but not stalls.

However, moveable premises may be required to register separately where they are used within a *market area* for the qualifying five day period by a person other than the controller of the market.

Moveable premises may also give rise to a requirement to register permanent premises if the permanent premises are used for a food business if the reason of keeping the moveable premises there.

Two or more Food Businesses within the same Permanent Premises

Where two or more permanent premises carrying on a food business are contained within one set of larger premises, the regulations require the registration of each of the smaller premises rather than the single larger premises.

Making the Application

1–55

The duty to register falls upon the Proprietor of the food business in respect of the individual premises. In the case of the premises which are used for the purposes of two or more food businesses the duty to register falls upon the person who permits the premises to be so used. A standard form is

---

[54] See *ante*, the Duty to Register, para. 1–52.

prescribed by the Regulations for use by applicants. Provided that the application has been properly made, the Registration Authority has a duty to register the premises within 28 days of receipt of the application.

It is unlawful to use premises for the purposes of a food business unless they have been registered or an application has been lodged at least 28 days before the first day premises are to be used for that purpose.

1–56 *Amendments to the Register*

Changes either in the identity of the Proprietor of the food business or in the nature of the food business carried on must be notified to the Registration Authority.[55] Such information must be notified at the latest within 28 days of the relevant change.

The Registration Authority also has a duty to register any relevant changes which have come to its notice other than by way of the requirement imposed by regulation 7(1) or 7(2) and the Proprietor must be given 28 days prior notice of the intention to make such an alteration by the Registration Authority. In these circumstances the Proprietor is entitled to make representations which must be considered by the Registration Authority.

Registration can continue for a limited period of time following the death of a person who is registered in respect of any premises. The registration continues for the benefit of the deceased's personal representative or widow or any other member of his family for a period up to three months after the death, or for such longer period as may be allowed by the Enforcement Authority.[56]

1–57 *Exceptions to the Requirement to Register*

There are a large number of exceptions to the general duty to register and there seems to be no common factor uniting all of the different exceptions. In those circumstances we simply reproduce here the list of exceptions set out in regulation 3.

Premises where the only commercial operation is carried out in regulation to food are:

[55] reg. 7(1) and 7(2).
[56] s. 43.

— Killing game for food by way of sport or the non-retail sale of food from game killed;

— Taking fish for food, or the non-retail sale of food from fish taken there;

— Harvesting food in the course of horticulture or viticulture or arable farming or the cleaning, storing, packaging or the non-retail sale of food harvested there except where the packaging is in a form in which the food is to be sold by retail;

— Collecting honey from bees;

— Production or packing of eggs or the non-retail sale of eggs produced or packed there;

— Retail sale of food by means of an automatic vending machine;

— The supply of beverages or of biscuits, crisps, confectionery or other similar products ancillary to a business whose principle activity is not the sale of food;

— The supply of food in the course of a religious ceremony;

— The premises used only as a dairy or dairy farm;

— Premises used by a person carrying on a food business as a distributor within the meaning of the Milk and Dairies (General) Regulations 1959;[57]

— Premises used as a slaughterhouse;

— Premises licensed as a slaughterhouse under regulation 12 of the Poultry, Meat (Hygiene) Regulations 1976[58];

— Premises used as export cutting premises, an export cold store or a transhipment centre approved under the regulation 4 of the Fresh Meat, Export (Hygiene and Inspection) Regulations 1987[59];

— An establishment preparing meat products for export to another Member State of the European Community;

— Premises controlled by a voluntary organisation or the trustees of a charity and used only for such purposes where no food other than dry ingredients for the preparation of beverages, sugar, biscuits, potato crisps or other similar products is stored for sale;

— Premises at which no food is intended for sale for human consumption is present and no relevant moveable premises are ordinarily kept. Premises where food is stored for sale or prepared for sale and

[57] S.I. 1959 No. 227.
[58] S.I. 1976 No. 1209.
[59] S.I. 1987 No. 2237. (This has been revoked by S.I. 1992 No. 2037).

it is intended that the sale will take place only in the event of an emergency or disaster;
— Premises certified under section 54(4) of the Food Safety Act 1990 (premises which in the interests of national security should not be subject to general powers of entry under section 32);
— Domestic premises which are used for the purposes of a food business where the proprietor does not reside there and the business does not consist of or include the peeling of shrimps or prawns.
— Domestic premises used for the purposes of a food business where the proprietor of the business does reside there but the only commercial operation in relation to food is the sale of food and the provision of accommodation in not more than three bedrooms or the sale or preparation of sale of honey or for horticultural or viticultural produce harvested on the premises.

The Food Premises (Registration) Amendment Regulations 1993[60] added the following category of premises:

— Domestic premises used for the purposes of a food business for the sale of food ancillary to the provision of child minding facilities. For these purposes the words "child minder" has the meaning given by section 71 of the Children Act 1989.

1–58   *The Form of the Register*

Regulations 5 and 6 prescribe that the information provided in accordance with the Regulations should be kept in two distinct parts; general information and a supplementary record.

— *The general information* part should contain the name and address of the premises together with the name of the business and particular nature of the business.

---

[60] S.I. 1993 No. 2022.

— *The supplementary record* is to be kept separate from the general part of the register or other information provided on the prescribed form of application.

Access to the Register   1–59

The *general information* part of the register must be kept open at all reasonable times for inspection by the public, a constable or any Authorised Officer of a Food Authority or the Minister. Copies of the entries in this part of the register may be provided and charges may be imposed for the provision of such copies.

The *supplementary record* is not open to inspection by the public but may be inspected at all reasonable times by the other persons referred to above. Again, copies may be supplied to those entitled to inspect.

Offences   1–60

Regulation 8 provides for a number of offences in connection with the Regulation provisions:

(a) using premises without having been registered;

(b) permitting premises to be used for the purposes of two or more businesses without having registered;

(c) failure to supply information in relation to change of proprietor or change in the nature of the food business;

(d) using premises which should be registered for the purposes of keeping relevant moveable premises there without having registered;

(e) knowingly furnishing false information;

(f) intentionally or recklessly disclosing information supplied to a registration authority otherwise than in the performance of his duty.

All offences are triable summarily only. In the case of (a), (b), (c) and (d) above the maximum penalty is level 3 on the standard scale, (currently £400). In the case of (e) and (f) above, the maximum penalty is level 5 on the standard scale (currently £5,000).

1–61 *Defences*

A specific defence to (f) above is provided by regulation 8(7) if a person charged in relation to a disclosure of information contained in the supplementary record[61] can show that he did not know and had no reasonable grounds to suspect that the person to whom disclosure was made was not a person to whom the disclosure could lawfully be made.

The more general "due diligence" defence[62] contained in section 21(1) of the FSA is also made available in connection with offences (a), (b), (c) and (d) above.

1–62 MINISTERIAL POWERS

Section 13 of the FSA introduces a new power to give effect to controls which had previously operated within the industry on a voluntary basis. A similar power exists in section 1 of the Food and Environment Protection Act 1985. This power allows a designating authority (a Minister) to make an Emergency Prohibition Order where circumstances exist which are likely to create a hazard to human health through human consumption of food.

It is not anticipated that the powers would ever be exercised in any situation other than one involving contamination or a food "scare" on a national basis where voluntary controls had failed to be applied uniformly in the first instance. No Code of Practice has been published under section 40 of the FSA in relation to these powers.

1–63 Emergency Control Orders

Section 13(1) empowers the Minister to prohibit commercial operations with respect to food, food sources or contact materials of any class or description. The power may be exercised if it appears to the Minister that the carrying out of such operations involves or may involve an imminent risk to health.

---

[61] See above.
[62] See *post*, para. 3–02.

For the purposes of this section, the term "the Minister" is defined in section 4(2) of the FSA in relation to England and Wales as the Minister of Agriculture Fisheries and Food or the Secretary of State.

There is no fetter to the exercise of the Minister's discretion, save those which usually apply to any exercise of executive authority (*i.e.* that the discretion must be exercised reasonably, taking all relevant considerations into account and excluding all irrelevant considerations).

The power is exercised by means of an Order issued by the Minister, and the power to make the Order is exercisable by statutory instrument.[63]

Section 13(3) provides some flexibility in the exercise of this function, by permitting the Minister to consent to the carrying out of anything which has been prohibited by such an Order.

Ancillary to the Order itself is a power contained in section 13(5)(a) to enable the Minister to issue such directions as appear to him to be necessary for the purpose of preventing the carrying out of a prohibited commercial operation (*e.g.* by directing that certain foods should be destroyed, or not used for the purposes of human consumption).

A further ancillary power is contained in section 13(5)(b) entitling the Minister to do anything which appears to him to be necessary or expedient for the same purpose (*e.g.* by prohibiting imports of certain foods or closing down certain premises).

Offences 1–64

Two offences are created by section 13 of the FSA. First, the offence of knowingly contravening an Emergency Control Order.[64] Secondly, the offence of failing to comply with a Direction under section 13(5)(a). As to these offences, and potential defences, see *post*.[65]

Recovery of costs 1–65

In a provision which bears some similarity to provisions in environmental legislation, section 13(7) empowers the Minister to recover any costs reasonably incurred by him as a result of the failure of any person to comply with an Order or Direction under section 13.

---

[63] FSA 1990, s. 48(2).
[64] *Ibid.*, s. 13(2).
[65] See *post*, para. 2–15..

The costs may only be recovered from the person whose failure to comply with the Order or Direction caused the Minister to take the appropriate action for which the costs are to be recovered.

1–66 Other Ministerial Powers

Section 6(3) of the FSA provides that Ministers may take over the execution of any duties which are normally carried out by Food Authorities by virtue of their statutory duty under section 6(2) of the FSA. Throughout the Act, powers are made available to Ministers to make Regulations in the discharge of the functions of the Act.

Section 16 enables Ministers to make regulations in relation to matters affecting food safety and consumer protection, *e.g.* regulating the use of specific products/processors, imposing requirements as to labelling/advertising.

Ministers are empowered by section 17 of the FSA to make regulations to give effect to their European Union obligations including measures which are of direct applicability.

Regulations under section 18 of the FSA may be made in relation to the prohibition of commercial operations with respect to particular classes of food, *e.g.* novel foods and genetically modified food sources. Orders may be made under section 25 of the Act by Ministers requiring certain classes of persons to provide information/assistance to persons who may be specified in the Orders, *e.g.* officers investigating specific types of cases.

The provisions relating to the taking of samples and analysis thereof may be supplemented or modified by regulations made under section 31 of the Act.

In the event that a Minister is satisfied that a Food Authority has failed to discharge its duties under the Act and such a failure is affecting the general interests of consumers, then under section 42 of the FSA, the Minister may empower another Food Authority to discharge that duty in place of the authority which is in default.

Regulations may be provided under section 45 of the FSA to allow Food Authorities to impose charges in respect of the discharge of their various responsibilities under the Act, *e.g.* in relation to the provision of food hygiene training under section 23 of the FSA or in relation to the registration and licensing provisions under section 19 of the FSA.

It should be noted that in respect of any regulations made by Ministers under the Act, apart from regulations made under sections 17 or 18, a statutory duty is imposed on the Minister under section 48(4) to consult with such organisations as appear to the relevant Minister to be representing those interests likely to be substantially affected by the proposed regulations.

Chapter 2
Prosecution and Offences Under the Food Safety Act

THE POWER TO PROSECUTE
2–01

The Food Authorities general powers of inspection and enforcement are given teeth by the various offences and powers to prosecute created by the FSA. The Food Authorities are under a statutory duty to enforce the provisions of the FSA by virtue of section 6 of the Act. Section 6(5) of the Act enables Authorities to take proceedings and to prosecute persons who offend against the provisions of the FSA. If an offence is proved and a conviction results then the courts have power to impose severe penalties by which a fine or imprisonment may be imposed and in certain circumstances to prohibit proprietors or managers of food businesses from participating in the management of any food business or any food business class or description specified by order of the court.[1] It is therefore in the interests of the proprietors, managers and operators of food businesses to co-operate with the Food Authority. Equally, it is clear from the FSA and the Codes of Practice that not every breach of the FSA will result in prosecution, but rather that criminal proceedings are the ultimate sanction available to the Food Authority in respect of offences under the FSA committed by those involved in the food trade and industry.

---

[1] See FSA 1990, s. 11(4).

2–02 THE DECISION TO PROSECUTE

Unlike the position in Scotland where a decision whether or not to prosecute can only be taken by the Procurator Fiscal, in England and Wales the Food Authorities themselves take the decision to prosecute and themselves have power to initiate and prosecute criminal proceedings. By section 6 of the FSA the Food Authorities in England and Wales are also the Enforcement Authorities. The Food Authorities in England and Wales therefore have the twofold responsibility of policing the provisions of the FSA and prosecuting offenders. It is plain both from the FSA and the Codes of Practice issued under section 40 of the Act that the legislative framework does not contemplate prosecution in each case where the provisions of the FSA have been breached or ignored. It is the important role of the Food Authority to liaise and offer advice to operators of food businesses in the area. So much is clear from the Codes of Practice which emphasise the need for a consultative and co-operative approach between the operators of food businesses and all others concerned in the food chain both in the local area and nationally. This consultative and co-operative approach should not only extend to those participating in the food trade and industry and the various Food Authorities but should also extend between county and district councils charged with differing responsibilities under the FSA. The emphasis on a consultative and co-operative approach is exemplified by section 23 of the FSA which expressly envisages the Food Authorities providing training courses in food hygiene to all persons involved in food businesses whether as proprietors, employees or otherwise.

The legislation therefore places an onus on the Authority to weigh carefully the decision to prosecute before any proceedings are initiated. The Code of Practice No. 2–Legal Matters indicates that the Authority should refer to the Code for Crown Prosecutors for guidance when considering a criminal prosecution. Further, Code of Practice No. 2 sets out factors which should be considered in each case before the decision to prosecute is made. The listed factors are:

(a) "the seriousness of the alleged offence;
(b) the previous history of the party concerned;
(c) the likelihood of the defendant being able to establish the due diligence defence;
(d) the ability of any important witness and their willingness to co-operate;

(e) the willingness of the party to prevent the recurrence of the problems;

(f) The probable public benefit of the prosecution and the importance of the case, *e.g.* whether it might establish legal precedent in other companies or in other geographical areas;

(g) whether other action, such as issuing a formal caution in accordance with Home Office Circular 59/1990 or improvement notice or imposing a prohibition, would be more appropriate or effective;

(h) any explanation offered by the affected company."

It is important to note that these factors are not exhaustive. All the circumstances in each particular case should be weighed before criminal proceedings are set in motion.

ALTERNATIVE MEASURES

2–03

The Food Authority has a range of measures it may take as an alternative to prosecution to ensure compliance with the legislation. Advice or an informal warning could be given. A formal caution in accordance with Home Office Circular 59/1990 could be issued. An informal improvement notice[2] or improvement notice under section 10 having statutory force could be appropriate. Sometimes a Prohibition Notice or Order may need to be imposed.

Such measures may become necessary from time to time and would routinely arise from the programmed systems of inspection of food businesses which the Act envisages and which the Food Authority should undertake. These measures short of prosecution can be utilised to cure any infringement of the FSA provisions and prevent any future occurrence or breach. In this way compliance with the legislation is achieved voluntarily through consultation and co-operation without resort to criminal prosecution. If an operator of a food business fails voluntarily to comply with an Improvement or Prohibition Notice then an offence is committed and the criminal sanction takes effect. If the operator of a food business has committed a serious offence, has a poor record of compliance with the legislation, is unco-operative and/or is unwilling to take remedial action then criminal proceedings may be appropriate. Save in exceptional circumstances it is submitted that in the absence of demonstrable culpability and a

---

[2] See Code of Practice No. 2–Legal Matters, s. 6.

want of due diligence the criminal prosecution of a food business operator with an ordinarily good record of compliance will rarely be appropriate.

For further guidance as to when it is appropriate to institute criminal proceedings see *Smedleys* v. *Breed* [1974] 2 All E.R. 21 especially at pp. 32–33 where Viscount Dilhorne said:

> "In cases where it is apparent that a prosecution does not serve the general interests of consumers, the justices may think fit, if they find that the Act has been contravened, to grant an absolute discharge."

2–04 OFFENCES RELATING TO FOOD SAFETY

In relation to all prosecutions which relate to food safety, it is important to remember the statutory presumption contained in section 3 of the FSA that any food which is commonly used for human consumption shall be presumed to have been intended for sale for human consumption until the contrary is proved.

2–05 Rendering Food Injurious to Health (*section 7*)

This provision substantially reproduces the provisions of the offence which formed section 1 of the Food Act 1984 (now repealed).

The constituent elements of the offence involve:

1. Rendering food injurious to health;
2. By means of

   — adding anything to the food;
   — using anything as an ingredient of the food;
   — taking any constituent element from the food;
   — subjecting the food to any other process or treatment.

3. With the intent that it shall be sold for human consumption.

The section provides assistance as to what constitutes "injury" in relation to health. In section 7(3) "Injury" is defined to include any impairment to health whether permanent or temporary.

Further assistance is also given as to the interpretation of the phrase "Injurious to Health". In considering whether the adulterated food is injurious to health, not only should the probable effect of the food on the health of the consumer be taken into account, but also the probable cumulative effect on the health of a person consuming that food in ordinary quantities.[3] This latter provision avoids any possibility of a successful defence on the basis that the adulteration complained of was a single incident and taken in isolation was unlikely to be injurious to health.

It should be noted that there must be some positive act on the part of the defendant to *render* the food injurious to health. A mere sale or supply of food which is in that state would not amount to an offence under section 7, although it may possibly be an offence under sections 8 or 14.[4]

There is no requirement that the act of adulteration be malicious in any way. The section would therefore appear to cover acts which are either deliberate or accidental.

Selling Food not Complying with Food Safety Requirements (*section 8*)   2–06

This section of the Act introduces two completely new offences of either:

1. Selling for human consumption offering, exposing or advertising for such sale, possessing for the purpose of such sale or possessing for the preparation for such sale; or
2. Depositing with or consigning to any other person for the purpose of such sale or preparation for such sale.

any food which fails to comply with food safety requirements.

An exclusive definition of a failure to comply with food safety requirements is given in section 8(2) of the FSA as:

1. Food which has been rendered injurious to health;
2. Food which is unfit for human consumption;
3. Food which is so contaminated that it would not be reasonable to expect it to be used for human consumption in that state.

A number of statutory presumptions are important in relation to these offences under section 8:   2–07

(a) The extended meaning given to "Sale" in section 2(1) to include a supply in the course of a business;
(b) If the food which fails to comply with food safety requirements forms part of a larger batch of food, then the whole of that batch is

---

[3] FSA 1990, s. 7(2).
[4] See *post*, paras. 2–06 and 2–16.

presumed to fail likewise. This is particularly important in relation to the power to seize contaminated food under section 9 of the FSA;

(c) Any animal or part thereof or product thereof which has been slaughtered or has been brought into a knackers yard is deemed to be unfit for human consumption;

(d) The definition of "Injurious to Health" contained in section 7(2)[5] applies equally to food which has been rendered injurious to health for the purposes of an offence under this section.

2–08 Contravention of a Seizure Notice (section 9(3))

Where an Authorised Officer of a Food Authority carries out an inspection of food and finds that the food fails to comply with the food safety requirements[6] (see section 8(2) FSA above) then he may give notice to the person in charge of that food that the food or any part of it:

1. shall not be used for human consumption; and
2. shall not be removed except to some specific place

Any person who *knowingly* contravenes the requirements of such a Notice commits an offence. The person committing the offence need not be the person upon whom the Notice was served. However, because of the need to prove that the defendant knew of the contents of the notice, the prosecution must show that the Notice was brought to the attention of the defendant in some way. It may be sufficient to prove that the defendant "turned a blind eye" to the existence of the notice and its requirements, as "knowledge" can be imputed by deliberately closing one's eyes to the relevant circumstances.[7]

2–09 Failure to Comply with an Improvement Notice (*section 10(2)*)

This subsection provides that *any person* who fails to comply with an Improvement Notice shall be guilty of an offence. The phrase "any

---

[5] See *ante.*
[6] See FSA s. 8(2) *ante.*
[7] See *Atwal* v. *Massey* [1971] 3 All E.R. 881.

person" in this context appears to be misleading, as the Notice itself can only legally be served on the proprietor of the business.[8]

Note, however, that the relevant Code of Practice provides that a copy of the Notice should be received by the person who is responsible for taking the appropriate action required by the Improvement Notice.

Section 10(1) also specifies that the Notice must require the *Proprietor* to take the measures set out in the Notice. In all the circumstances, it is submitted that only the Proprietor of the business can face prosecution for failure to comply with the terms of the Notice. It should be remembered that section 39(2) of the FSA effectively suspends the period of the improvement notice until such time as any pending appeal has been disposed of/withdrawn/struck out.

Failure to Comply with a Prohibition Order (*section 11(5)*)

2–10

The provisions of section 11(5) of the FSA *make it an offence for any person* to knowingly contravene a Prohibition Order. Although in this section, the Notice must be served on the *Proprietor* of the business,[9] the Notice must also be affixed to the premises in a conspicuous position.[10]

In these circumstances, it may be easier for the prosecution to pursue proceedings against a person other than the Proprietor, especially where the notice, when affixed to the premises, would have been visible to all persons attending at the premises who might have been affected by the appropriate prohibition.

The inclusion of the word "knowingly"[11] implies that the defendant must have been aware of the provisions of the notice. It would be important therefore where the defendant is a person other than the Proprietor, that the prosecution can prove that the Notice was properly affixed to the premises in accordance with section 11(5)(b), and that the notice remained *in situ*. The Code of Practice renders some assistance in this regard, as it suggests that the food authority should arrange for periodic checks to be made on the notice to establish that it is still there.

---

[8] See FSA s. 10(1).
[9] See FSA s. 11(5)(a).
[10] See FSA s. 11(5)(b).
[11] As to the meaning of "knowingly" in relation to this section, see above. See above also as to where the Order ceases to have effect.

2-11 Contravention of an Emergency Prohibition Notice (*section 12(5)*)

The offence under section 12(5) is in very similar terms to that under section 11(5). It becomes an offence for any person to knowingly contravene the provisions of an Emergency Prohibition Notice.

As with the provisions of section 11 of the FSA, the Food Authority is required to serve a copy of the Notice on the Proprietor of the business and also to affix a copy of the Notice on the premises.[12]

It should be remembered that the Emergency Prohibition Notice has a finite period of existence; either a period of three days beginning with the date of service of the Notice (if no application is made for an Emergency Prohibition Order), or the date on which the Emergency Prohibition Order is determined by the court or abandoned. It would be impossible to bring a prosecution for an offence alleged to have taken place outside those time limits.

2-12 Failure to comply with an Emergency Prohibition Order (*section 12(6)*)

The terms of this offence are very similar to those contained in section 11(5) of the FSA. Any person who knowingly contravenes the Emergency Prohibition Order shall be guilty of an offence under section 12(6) of the FSA.

Once more, the FSA requires both the service of the Order on the Proprietor of the business, and that the Order be affixed to the premises.

The Order ceases to have effect only on the issue of a Certificate of Satisfaction by the Food Authority.[13]

2-13 Contravention of an Emergency Control Order (*section 13(2)*)

The basic offence under this section is one of knowingly contravening an Emergency Control Order.

Orders under this section which are made by Ministers are given legal effect by statutory instrument.[14]

---

[12] See FSA, ss. 12(1) and 12(5).
[13] See *ante*, FSA s. 12(8).
[14] See FSA s. 48(2).

There is no requirement in the FSA that the relevant Order should be served on any particular person or affixed to any particular premises. As the purpose of the section is to give statutory effect to a process which already exists on a voluntary basis within the food industry, the Emergency Control Orders will operate on an industry-wide basis and will relate to particular classes of food stuffs rather than individual premises or persons.

Given therefore that the relevant Order will be created by statutory instrument, everyone upon whom the Order will have effect will be presumed to have knowledge of the Order.

The element of "knowingly" committing this offence therefore will refer to the defendant's knowledge of the prohibited act or operation itself. It will not be a defence to claim lack of knowledge of the existence of the Order.

Statutory Defence   2–14

Quite apart from the general defence of due diligence under section 21(1) of the FSA which would be available to any defendant charged with an offence under section 13(2) of the FSA, a specific statutory defence is also available under section 13(4) of the FSA. Section 13(4) of the FSA provides that it shall be a defence for the defendant to prove:

  (a) That ministerial consent had been given to the breach of the Order under section 13(3) of the FSA; and

  (b) That any condition that had been attached to the ministerial consent had been complied with.

As is the case with all statutory defences, the burden of proof on the defendant is on the balance of probabilities, rather than the more onerous prosecution burden of beyond all reasonable doubt.

Failure to comply with Ministerial Direction (*section 13(6)*)   2–15

Directions may be given by the Minster under section 13(5)(a) of the FSA for the purpose of prohibiting commercial operations to which an Order made under section 13(1) of the FSA applies. A failure to comply with such directions is an offence under section 13(6) of the FSA. No mental element is required to establish the offence, which would seem to be absolute, subject only to the general defence of due diligence contained in section 21(1) of the FSA.

2–16 OFFENCES RELATING TO CONSUMER PROTECTION

Sale to the Purchaser's prejudice (*section 14*)

Section 14(1) of the FSA reproduces almost exactly the offence which was previously contained in section 2 of the Food Act 1984. The latest phraseology for this offence is that:

> "Any person who sells to the purchasers prejudice any food which is not of the nature or substance or quality demanded by the purchaser shall be guilty of an offence."

This offence has a distinguished history and can be traced back through corresponding legislation for many years. In consequence, a large body of case law has built up around the interpretation of the offence which is equally relevant to section 14(1) of the FSA today.

It is important to remember the extended definition of "sale" contained in section 2(1)(a) of the FSA to include the supply of food, otherwise than on sale, in the course of a business. This definition is further extended by section 14(2) of the FSA to include a statutory presumption that the reference to sale should be a reference to sale for human consumption. This offence appears to be the most widely used by prosecuting authorities when considering complaints in relation to contamination of food by foreign bodies.

2–17   The words "nature or substance or quality" are not necessarily mutually exclusive but any charge or summons which includes a reference to two or more of those factors will be bad for duplicity.[15]

There is judicial authority for the proposition that there is a large area of common ground between the three words "nature/substance/quality" and it is really for the prosecution to decide on any particular set of facts whether it is the nature or the substance or the quality of the food which has been affected.[16] In practice, whichever word is used in the charge or summons to describe the food complained of is unlikely to materially affect the prosecution or defence case.

It must also be shown that the person who sold the food acted in a manner prejudicial to the purchaser. The purchaser cannot be prejudiced if

---

[15]   See r. 12 of the Magistrates Court Rules 1981.
[16]   See, *e.g. Bastin* v. *Davies* [1952] K.B. 579.

the defect/contamination in the product which is sold is clearly brought to the notice of the purchaser at the time of the sale.

False description/advertisement/presentation of food (*section 15*)

2–18

This section recreates in broadly similar terms, the provisions of the offences created by section 6 of the Food Act 1984. As the terminology of the new offences under section 15 is close to that used in section 6 of the Food Act 1984, the case law in respect of the older offences may be equally applicable to the new ones.

The section breaks down into three separate subsections which create three different types of offences. Offences under this section may also constitute an offence contrary to section 1 of the Trade Descriptions Act 1968.

False/Misleading Description (section 15(1))

2–19

It is an offence for any person to give with any food sold by him or displayed with any food offered for sale or exposed for sale or possessed for sale by him a label which:

(i) falsely describes the food; or
(ii) is likely to mislead as to the nature or substance or quality of the food.

There is no statutory definition as to what might constitute a "label" for the purposes of this offence, although subsection 15(1) of the FSA includes a label "whether or not attached to or printed on the wrapper or container."

The usual statutory presumption as to the extended meaning of "sale" applies.[17] A further presumption is included in section 15(5) of the FSA that references to sale shall be construed as "sale for human consumption."

Section 15(4) of the FSA allows the court to find the offence proved despite the fact that the label contained an accurate statement of the composition of the food. This provision would cover the situation where a specious claim might be made for the food, *e.g.* "promotes hair growth" whilst the label also contained a full and accurate description of the ingredients in the product.

---

[17] See FSA, s. 2.

The question as to whether or not the label is likely to mislead is a question of fact to be decided on a test of reasonableness, *i.e.* what does the ordinary man understand by the language?[18]

2–20 *Publication of False/Misleading Material (section 15(2))*

It is an offence for any person to publish or be party to the publication of an advertisement which:

   (i)   falsely describes food; or
  (ii)   is likely to mislead as to the nature or substance or quality of the food.

As with the previous offence, section 15(2) of the FSA recreates more or less exactly the provisions of section 6(2) Food Act 1984.

The subsection also provides that the advertisement must not be a label given or displayed as mentioned in section 15(1) of the FSA. Clearly, a prosecution under section 15(1) would preclude a prosecution under section 15(2) of the FSA. Again, the test of whether the advertisement is likely to mislead is that of whether the ordinary man would be misled.

2–21 *Misleading Presentation of Food (section 15(3))*

It is an offence to sell, offer, expose for sale or possess for the purpose of sale any food, the presentation of which is likely to mislead as to the nature or substance or quality of the food.

This offence was not previously contained in the corresponding legislation under section 6 of the Food Act 1984 although it is covered in similar terms by regulation 4 of the Food Labelling Regulations 1984.[19]

"Presentation" is specifically defined in section 53(1) of the FSA in relation to food as to include "the shape, appearance and packaging of the food, the way in which the food is arranged when exposed for sale and the setting in which the food is displayed with a view to sale."

---

[18] See, *e.g. Concentrated Food Limited* v. *Champ* [1944] K.B. 342.
[19] S.I. 1984 No. 1305.

This definition is not exclusive, although any form of labelling or advertising is specifically excluded. A similar definition of "presentation" was adopted in the Food Labelling Regulations 1984.[20]

OFFENCES RELATING TO FOOD AUTHORITY FUNCTIONS

2–22

Unlawful disclosure of information

Persons who are in a privileged position to gain information about food businesses because of powers conferred on them by the FSA risk severe penalties for any breaches of confidence.

There are two separate provisions which create offences of this nature:

Information Relating to Trade Secrets

2–23

Section 32(7) of the FSA reproduces in similar terms an offence which existed in section 87(5) of the Food Act 1984. The offence under the FSA involves the disclosure to any persons of any information obtained in premises with regard to a trade secret obtained by a person who enters premises by virtue of the power of entry granted by section 32(1) of the FSA, or a warrant issued under section 32(2) of the FSA.

No definition of "trade secrets" is given in the FSA although it would clearly have to relate to information which was peculiar to the organisation whose premises were entered.

Note that the offence is not made out if the disclosure is made in the performance of the persons duty, *e.g.* by issuing an Emergency Prohibition Notice or Improvement Notice containing information relating to a trade secret.

Note also that no damage or loss resulting from the disclosure has to be proved. Mere disclosure itself to any person, even another Authorised Officer, would suffice to prove the offence provided the disclosure was outside the performance of the officer's duty.

---

[20] S.I. 1984 No. 1305.

2–24 *Information Obtained by Ministerial Direction*

Under section 25(1) of the FSA, the Ministers may make Orders requiring persons carrying on certain classes of business to furnish information to persons specified in the Order. Such Orders may be made by the Ministers for the purpose of exercising their functions under the Act.

Section 25(3) of the FSA creates an offence of disclosing such information which relates to an individual business without the consent in writing of the person carrying on the business except:

   (i)   following the directions of the Minister for the purposes of the FSA or any Community obligation; or

  (ii)   for the purposes of any proceedings for an offence against the Order or any report of those proceedings.

Clearly, the written consent of the person carrying on the business concerned would be a complete defence to a summons or charge brought under this section.

The information which is disclosed must be peculiar to an individual business and must not refer to the general operation of the class of businesses specified in the Order.

2–25 **Obstruction of an Officer**

"Any person who intentionally obstructs any person in the execution of this Act . . . shall be guilty of an offence."[21] The wording of this offence corresponds almost exactly with a similar offence contained in section 91 of the Food Act 1984.

The significant difference between the two offences is the change in the description of the mental element in the offence from the word "wilfully" in the 1984 Act to the word "intentionally" in the FSA.

In the context of cases involving obstruction of officers acting in the execution of their duty (including cases on a similarly worded statute under section 51(3) of the Police Act 1964) the word "wilfully" had come to connote merely the intention to do the act of obstruction which was

---

[21] See FSA, s. 33(1)(a).

complained of, intending that an obstruction should result. The reason for carrying out the act of obstruction is irrelevant.[22]

Clearly, by wording the new offence in the FSA to include the word **2–26** "intentionally" some different effect in respect of the mental element must have been intended by Parliament. It is submitted therefore that the use of the word "intentionally" in this offence means the prosecution must show not only that the defendant intended to do the act complained of, but also that he intended that the act should amount to an *unlawful* obstruction.

If the defendant reasonably believed that he was entitled to act in the way he did, *e.g.* if he reasonably thought that the officer who was obstructed was not an Authorised Officer, or was not acting in the execution of the Act, then it is submitted that he would be entitled to an acquittal.

The prosecution must also be able to show that at the time of the obstruction, the officer was acting "in the execution of the Act". This phrase would include acting in the execution of any Regulations, Orders or Directions made under the Act.

Failing to give its assistance/information to an Officer

2–27

Section 33(1)(b) of the FSA provides that "any person who without reasonable cause fails to give to any person acting in the execution of this Act any assistance or information which that person might reasonably require of him for the performance of his functions under the Act" shall be guilty of an offence. This section would seem to infringe on the generally accepted right to silence of a potential defendant.

However, section 33(3) of the Food Safety Act provides specifically that nothing in section 33(1)(b) above shall be construed as requiring any person to answer any question or give any information which might incriminate him. A real conflict exists between the powers of Authorised Officers to request information under section 32(5) and (6) and the right against self-incrimination contained in section 33(3). In exercising his powers to request information or assistance under section 32, the Authorised Officer must be sure that the information or assistance is required in respect of evidence gathering for the purposes of breaches of the Act or regulations made thereunder, rather than in respect of a "due diligence" defence.

---

[22] See, *e.g. Lewis* v. *Cox* [1985] Q.B. 509.

2–28 OFFENCES BY BODIES CORPORATE

In certain circumstances, where an offence under the FSA has been committed by a corporate body, the senior officers of that Company may also become liable in respect of the same offence.

Section 36(1) FSA provides that:

> "any director, manager, secretary or other similar officer or any person purporting to act in that capacity . . . shall be deemed to be guilty of an offence proved to have been committed by a body corporate, if the offence is proved to have been committed with the consent or connivance of, or is attributable to neglect on the part of that person."

This offence is not of recent origin and is found in similar form in many other statutes.

Considerable case law has built up involving the question of how far down the company's ladder of management the responsibility for these criminal acts will extend. The words "director" and "secretary" of a company have a clear and obvious meaning. The meaning of the word "manager" is less clear.

The leading case on this point is *Tesco Supermarkets Limited* v. *Nattrass*[23] where it was held that the failings of a manager of a supermarket which was part of a national chain, could not render his employing company criminally liable as he was not a person in actual control of the company's operations who could be identified with the controlling mind and will of the company.

A more recent case under a similar provision of the Fire Precautions Act 1971 (section 23 thereof) provides a very clear guideline as to who should be criminally liable in these circumstances. In that case (*R.* v. *Boal*[24]) it was held that the intended scope of the Act was to fix with criminal liability only those who were in a position of real authority and who were responsible for putting proper procedures in place, *i.e. the decision makers within the Company who had both the power and responsibility to decide corporate policy and strategy*.

The courts have not been slow to exercise their functions in relation to offences committed by directors in these circumstances, and the scope of a

---

[23] [1972] A.C. 153.
[24] [1992] 1 Q.B. 591.

64

conviction of a director may also render him liable to disqualification as a director under section 2(1) of the Company Directors Act 1986. This section allows disqualification as a director in respect of any indictable offence connected with the promotion, formation, management or liquidation of a company.

TIME LIMITS FOR PROSECUTIONS   2–29

Section 34 of the FSA lays down strict time limits for bringing proceedings in relation to offences committed under the Food Safety Act. No proceedings in respect of any offences under the FSA apart from the two offences contained in section 33(1) of the FSA can be commenced after either:

    (a) three years from the commission of the offence; or
    (b) one year from its discovery by the prosecutor whichever is the earlier.

In the case of the two offences contrary to section 33(1), section 35(1) of the FSA indicates that those offences are of a purely summary nature, and can only be tried in a Magistrates Court. In those circumstances, the time limit imposed by section 127 of the Magistrates Court Act 1980 will apply. That section provides that a Magistrate Court cannot try a summons unless the summons was laid within six months from the time when the offence was committed.

PENALTIES   2–30

Section 35 of the FSA deals with punishment of offences committed under the FSA. Section 35(1) of the FSA provides that a person guilty of either of the offences under section 33(1) of the FSA shall be liable to a fine not exceeding level 5 on the standard scale or to imprisonment for a term not exceeding three months or both.

Level 5 on the standard scale involves a maximum fine of £5,000 following the raising of the statutory maxima on October 1, 1992 when section 17 of the Criminal Justice Act 1991 came into force.

Any offence committed under the Act apart from those under section 33(1) of the FSA attracts the following penalties:

"Conviction on Indictment—a fine or imprisonment for a maximum of two years or both.

Summary Conviction—a fine not exceeding the relevant amount or imprisonment for a maximum of six months or both."

In relation to Summary Conviction, the "relevant amount" means:

(a) £20,000 for offences under section 7, 8 or 14
(b) the statutory maximum (£5,000) for any other offence.

Apart from offences under section 33(1) of the FSA, all other offences under the FSA are indictable.

It must be remembered that under section 36 of the FSA, directors and similar officers of corporate bodies can be punished in the same way for the same offences as those committed by their companies.

Chapter 3
Statutory Defences

INTRODUCTION

In the event of a criminal prosecution the defendant may have a range of **3–01** defences available. The defences may be procedural or substantial. Not least of these may be the defence that no offence was committed or no offence has been proved by the authority to the required standard. The standard of proof is the criminal standard namely the court must be sure that the offence has been committed: the offence must be proved beyond all reasonable doubt. In many cases, however, the provisions of the FSA may have been obviously contravened. An offence may have been committed for example, by selling food not complying with food safety requirements contrary to section 8 of the FSA or by selling food, not of the nature, substance or quality demanded contrary to section 14 of the FSA. Such instances may include food which has become contaminated by a foreign object or substance rendering it unfit for human consumption. This would constitute an offence under section 8 of the Act.[1] Alternatively, a food product may be improperly cooked, processed or prepared. An obvious example may be the sale of under-cooked food. This would constitute an

---

[1] For the choice of whether a prosecution should be brought under s. 8 or s. 14 of the FSA. See Code of Practice No. 1–Responsibility for enforcement of the FSA 1990, ss. 7, 8 and 18.

offence under section 14 of the FSA.[2] Yet further an operator of a food business may present for sale food which is falsely presented or described. For example, an operator of a food business may present for sale a can of beans when the can contains peas or the operator may describe the product as "extra-virgin olive oil" when it is in reality simple olive oil. This would constitute an offence under section 15 of the FSA. In all these examples and in many other instances a statutory defence may be available to the operator of the food business.

3-02 **The Defence of Due Diligence/Act or Default of Another Person (*section 21*)**

The FSA provides a general statutory defence of due diligence under section 21. This is a new defence introduced for the purposes of FSA. It was not available in respect of a prosecution under the Food Act 1984. The defence is framed in similar terms to that which is available under section 24 of the Trade Descriptions Act 1968. Essentially section 21 of the FSA provides a statutory defence to persons charged with any offence under the Act providing that the person charged can prove that all reasonable precautions were taken and all due diligence exercised to avoid the commission of the alleged offence. The burden of proving the statutory defence rests with the person charged. The burden of proof is to the standard of civil proceedings. The defence must be established on the balance of probabilities. No conviction will result therefore if the person charged can prove that he *probably* took all reasonable precautions and exercised all due diligence to avoid the commission of the alleged offence.

The statutory defence, however, has two tiers. Section 21(1) of the FSA provides an all encompassing defence of due diligence. This may or may not include an assertion that the commission of the offence was caused by the act or default of another person or on reliance of information supplied by another person. The statutory defence under subsection (1) is of universal application. There is a second tier to the defence created by subsections (2)–(4). These subsections create "deemed defences" and apply only to offences under sections 8, 14 or 15 of the FSA. The "deemed defences" do not apply to persons charged who are involved in the preparation of food and/or its importation into Great Britain. It is necessary

---

[2] For the choice of whether a prosecution should be brought under s. 8 or s. 14 of the FSA. See Code of Practice No. 1–Responsibility for enforcement of the Food Safety Act 1990, ss. 7, 8 and 18.

therefore to consider the general defence under section 21(1) and the deemed defences under section 21(2)–(4) of the FSA separately.

General Defence of Due Diligence (*section 21(1)*) 3–03

Section 21(1) of the FSA provides:

> "In any proceedings for an offence under any preceding provision of this Part (in this section referred to as 'the relevant provision'), it shall, subject to subsection (5) be a defence for the person charged to prove that he took all reasonable precautions and exercised all due diligence to avoid the commission of the offence by himself or by a person under his control."

This section makes it plain that an operator of a food business would not be liable for every offence committed by himself or an employee or person acting under his control. Clearly, circumstances may arise when the defendant himself or an employee or person acting under his control commits an act or default which results in a breach of the provisions of the FSA. No conviction will result provided the defendant can establish that all reasonable precautions and all due diligence was exercised to avoid the commission of the offence by himself or by a person under his control. This will primarily involve the defendant proving that there were adequate systems of work, or organisation, supervision and training to prevent the occurrence of the offence. Each case will need to be considered in the context of its own facts and all the circumstances of each case should be taken into account in considering what was or was not reasonable. Aspects of best practice in systems of work are discussed in more detail below. It is important to note that whilst the Act uses the words "all reasonable precautions" and "all due diligence" this is not an absolute standard nor is it a standard of perfection. The defendant is required to act to the limit of what is reasonable in all the circumstances. If the system has operated faultlessly over a prolonged period or a period of years or has been inspected by the Food Authority without criticism or the need for action then it is likely that the system is sound and if on a single occasion an offence is committed then such is likely to be as a result of an isolated failure attributable to a freak occurrence (see *Carrick District Council* v. *Taunton Vale Meat Traders Ltd* (*The Times*, February 15, 1994)). In these circumstances if an operator of a food business can establish that such an offence occurred notwithstanding the institution and maintenance of an adequate system of control, then no conviction should result. Further, in such circumstances where an isolated offence has occurred against a background of successful operation then a criminal prosecution would seldom be appropriate. It is therefore important for operators of food businesses to institute and maintain adequate procedures and systems to satisfy the statutory test and the reader is referred to the section on Best Practice below.

3-04 The Deemed Defences of Due Diligence (*section 21(2)–(4)*)

Subsections (2)–(4) of section 21 are to protect from conviction the operator of a food business who has committed an offence under sections 8, 14 or 15 unwittingly owing to the act or default of a third party or as a result of relying on information supplied by a third party. This is made clear by the preceding section 20 which states:

> "Where the commission by any person of an offence under any of the preceding provisions of this Part is due to an act or default of some other person, that other person shall be guilty of the offence; and a person may be charged with and convicted of the offence by virtue of this section whether or not proceedings are taken against the first-mentioned person."

Thus even if the offence is in fact committed by one person, for example at the point of sale by selling food that is unfit for human consumption, then nonetheless, if the fault in reality lies with a third party that third party may be prosecuted even though he was a stranger to the commission of the offence. This is so even if the person who in fact committed the offence at the point of sale is neither charged with any offence nor is party to the criminal offence. In many instances therefore if the Food Authority after investigation of a complaint or offence discovers that a retailer has committed an offence but in reality the fault lies with the wholesaler or supplier or producer then proceedings can be brought directly against the wholesaler or supplier or producer. If however, the proceedings are brought against the person who committed the offence then it is open to that person to rely on the defence of due diligence under section 21 of the FSA and if appropriate to rely on the deemed defences under subsections (2)–(4).

3-05 In effect subsections (2)–(4) provide a short cut to the establishment of the defence of due diligence. The general defence of due diligence under section 21(1) would require the person charged to call such evidence as will establish on the balance of probabilities that he took all reasonable precautions and exercised all due diligence to avoid the commission of the offence whether by himself or by a person under his control. The requirements of proof under subsections (2)–(4) are more limited. The statutory defences under subsections (2)–(4) are not, however, available to all food businesses. Subsection (2) states:

> "(2) Without prejudice to the generality of subsection (1) above, a person charged with an offence under section 8, 14 or 15 above who neither—
> (a) prepared the food in respect of which the offence was alleged to have been committed; nor
> (b) imported it into Great Britain
> shall be taken to have established a defence provided by that subsection if he satisfies the requirements of sub-section (3) or (4) below."

Therefore, preparers of food and importers of food will not be able to rely on this Section which in any event is only a defence to offences under sections 8, 14 or 15 of the FSA. Section 53 of the Act assists in the definition/interpretation of the word "preparation". Section 53 provides that: **3–06**

> " 'Preparation', in relation to food, includes manufacture and any form of processing or treatment."

Section 53 of the Act further assists in the definition/interpretation of the word "treatment". Section 53 provides that:

> " 'Treatment' in relation to any food, includes subjecting it to heat or cold."

It is noteworthy that the general interpretations offered by section 53 are phrased inclusively and should not therefore be regarded as excluding other similar types of operation.

It seems plain that any form of cooking or refrigerated storage would be caught by the terms "preparation" and "treatment". Any food business operator who cooks or refrigerates food in respect of which an offence has been committed will not therefore be able to rely on the deemed statutory defences under subsections (2)–(4) of section 21 of the FSA. This restriction, however, relates to the preparation or importation of "the food in respect of which the offence is alleged to be committed". It does not therefore prevent an operator of the food business who is involved in the preparation of food or the importation of food into Great Britain from relying on the deemed statutory defence if the food in question was not food which the defendant prepared or imported. For example, a restaurateur can rely on the defence provided by these subsections in respect of a canned food product which has not been cooked or refrigerated by the defendant. Similarly, a storekeeper who stocks and sells refrigerated products as part of a general grocery business will not be able to rely on the defence provided by these subsections in respect of his frozen products but would in relation to his shelf stock. The apparent inclusion of refrigerated storage in the interpretation of "treatment", seems harsh in its effect, particularly on the smaller operator of a food business. For example, a grocery storekeeper may stock and sell many frozen items including processed meat or fish products and ice creams.

3–07   The extended meaning given to "treatment" by the Act would seem, for instance, to prevent an innocent storekeeper who sold an ice cream which was contaminated by a foreign object, from relying on the deemed statutory defence under section 21 (2) in answer to a prosecution under section 8. This is despite the fact that it may be obvious that the contamination occurred because of the fault of the manufacturer/processor of the ice cream. Thus, if a mechanical part of a processing machine is discovered in a can of peas sold by a storekeeper, he will be able to rely on the deemed statutory defences provided by subsections (2)–(4). On the other hand, if a mechanical part of a processing machine is discovered in a tub of ice cream refrigerated and sold by the storekeeper, he will not. This, at first, appears illogical and anomalous. Although the storekeeper could rely on the general defence of due diligence provided by section 21 (1), the onus of proof in satisfying that subsection is more onerous and wide ranging than the deemed offences under subsection (3)–(4). Subsection (3) of section 21 of the FSA provides that:

> "(3) the person satisfies the requirements of this subsection if he proves—
>
> (a) that the commission of the offence was due to an act or default of another person who was not under his control or to reliance on information supplied by such a person
>
> (b) that he carried out all such checks of the food in question as were reasonable in all the circumstances, or that it was reasonable in all the circumstances for him to rely on checks carried out by the person who supplied the food to him; and
>
> (c) that he did not know and had no reason to suspect at the time of the commission of the alleged offence that his act or omission would amount to an offence under the relevant provision."

Subsection (4) of section 21 provides that:

> "A person satisfies the requirements of this subsection if he proves—

(a) that the commission of the offence was due to an act or default of another person who was not under his control, or to reliance on information supplied by such a person;

(b) that the sale or intended sale of which the alleged offence consisted was not a sale or intended sale under his name or mark; and

(c) that he did not know, and could not reasonably have been expected to know, at the time of the commission of the alleged offence that his act or omission would amount to an offence under the relevant provision."

These subsections are considered separately below, but the narrower **3–08** wording of the two-limbed defence under subsections (3) and (4) is to be contrasted with the broader words of "all reasonable precautions" and "all due diligence" used to describe the measures which the defendant needs to satisfy if he is to establish the general defence of due diligence under section 21(1).

In reality the average storekeeper or smaller operator of the food business would rely exclusively on the checks carried out by the supplier of food to him and on information supplied to him by the supplier about the food and its condition. This would be particularly the case in respect of brand market leaders of food products with a national or international reputation. The storekeeper or smaller operator of the food business may simply accept delivery, keep in refrigerated stock and then sell the food product. It is submitted that it would not be reasonable for a storekeeper or a smaller operator of the food business to himself arrange or undertake inspections of the factories of his various suppliers of frozen food products. Likewise, it would not be reasonable to expect the storekeeper or smaller operator of the food business to himself break open or subject frozen food products to random destructive sampling. Any such frozen food products have tamper-proof seals or could not be refrigerated or sold once the packaging or seals had been broken or the food product exposed. If the same product had been canned, the same person could rely on the deemed statutory defences under subsections (3) and (4) which in the majority of cases could usually be satisfied. In the case of frozen food products it seems that the operator of the food business needs to satisfy more stringent tests under section 21(1). Although this may appear illogical and anomalous, it is submitted that the distinction of frozen food is deliberate. The reason for the apparent anomalous provisions relating to refrigerated storage seem to stress the importance of the ensuring proper refrigeration of food at every point in the food chain. Improper refrigeration of food would not only impair the standard and quality of many frozen food products but may also create a risk that food products may become unsafe or unfit for human consumption due to a lack of proper or adequate refrigeration.

3–09   The inclusion of refrigerated storage, therefore, imposes even on the smallest operator of the food business a duty to ensure *and be able to prove*, if necessary, that his refrigeration procedures satisfy all reasonable safety requirements. Plainly, in many cases, the Food Authority, after investigation of a complaint or an offence may choose to exercise its powers under section 20 of the FSA to prosecute the supplier directly. If, however, a prosecution is commenced against a retailer, he will not be able to rely on the deemed offences under subsections (2) and (4) in respect of frozen food but will need to prove that his refrigeration procedures are as safe as can reasonably be expected and that the measures taken were sufficient to satisfy the broader statutory test under section 21(1) of the Act.

3–10 # Act or Default of Another Person
(*section 21(3) & (4)*)

In the event that an operator of a food business can establish that he neither prepared nor imported the food in respect of which an offence is alleged to have been committed, then his burden of discharging the defence of due diligence is reduced if he can satisfy the criteria set out in any of the subsections (3) and (4) of section 21.

Subsections (3) and (4) each respectively contain three ingredients. Common to subsections (3) and (4) is the requirement under subsection (a) that the commission of the offence was due to an act or default of another person who is not under his control, or to reliance on the information supplied by such person. Thereafter, subsection (3) and (4) differ.

Subsection (3) in addition to proof of the first ingredient (a) requires proof of two other factors. First, that the defendant carried out all such checks of the food in question as was reasonable in all the circumstances, or that it was reasonable in all the circumstances for him to rely on checks carried out by the person who supplied the food. Secondly, and again in addition to the first requirement of subsection (3)(a), he must prove that he did not know and had no reason to suspect at the time of commission of the alleged offence that his act or omission would amount to an offence under the relevant provision.

In other words, if the defendant is to successfully rely on the statutory deemed defence under subsection (3), he must show:

1.   that the commission of the offence was not his fault; and

2. that he carried out all such checks on the food supplied to him as were reasonable in all the circumstances; and
3. that he was innocent in the commission of the offence, *i.e.* that the defendant "did not know and had no reason to suspect" that he was likely to commit an offence.

This subsection is likely to be relied on by a person who stocks and sells **3–11** food supplied to him by another person but under the defendant's own name or mark. For example, the food may not be labelled or marked as another person's product.

Subsection (4) contrasts with subsection (3) in that although subsection (a) is the same, the remaining two necessary ingredients contain different elements. Subsection (4)(b) applies in circumstances where a person charged has committed an offence, for example, by selling or presenting for sale food which was marketed under the name or make of another person. This will be commonplace. Significantly, the third ingredient of proof under subsection (4)(c) is different from its corresponding ingredient under subsection (3) in that it requires the defendant to prove that he was innocent in that he:

> "did not know and *could not reasonably have been expected to know*, at the time of commission of the alleged offence that his act or omission would amount to an offence . . . "
> (italics added for emphasis)

Subsection (4)(c) fixes the person with a degree of constructive knowledge whereas subsection (3)(c) does not. Subsections (3) and (4) will therefore be utilised in different circumstances.

Subsection (4) is likely to be the most frequently invoked subsection. In these circumstances, providing the person charged satisfies the three necessary ingredients, namely, that the commission of the offence was due to an act or default of another person, the defendant himself was innocent and that the sale or intended sale of the food was not a sale or intended sale under his label or mark then the person charged will escape liability and conviction. The most common instance is likely to be the storekeeper who sells or presents for sale a food product manufactured, processed or supplied by a third party under a brand name or mark.

Subsection (3) is most likely to be used by the larger operator of the food **3–12** business or larger storekeeper who stocks a range of products under his own name or mark but which in reality are supplied manufactured or processed by a third party. In this instance, the person charged will need to satisfy the court if he sells such food under his own name or mark that he carried out all such checks of the food in question as were reasonable in all the circumstances or that it was reasonable in all the circumstances for him to rely on checks carried out by the person who supplied food to him. This, for example, may involve the person charged in proving that he had some system of inspection of the food safety hygiene standards instituted and maintained by his third party supplier/manufacturer/processor. The wording of the section implies that in certain circumstances reliance could probably be placed (particularly in respect of the smaller operator of the food business) on checks carried out by the supplier/third party.

3–13 ## Requirement of Notice

It is a prerequisite for any person seeking to rely on any statutory defence under section 21 of the FSA which "involves the allegation that the commission of the offence was due to an act or default of another person" to serve a notice of his intention to do so on the Prosecutor/Enforcement Authority in accordance with section 21(5) of the Act. There is a time limit for service of the notice. Section 21(5) states that :

> "(5) If in any case the defence provided by subsection (1) above involves the allegation that the commission of the offence was due to an act or default of another person, or to reliance on information supplied by another person, the person charged shall not, without leave of the court, be entitled to rely on that defence unless—,
> (a) at least seven clear days before the hearing; and
> (b) where he has previously appeared before a Court in connection with the alleged offence, within one month of his first such appearance,
> he has served on the prosecutor a notice in writing giving such information identifying or assisting in the identification of that other person as was then in his possession."

Section 21(6) qualifies the time limit and states:

> "(6) In subsection (5) above any reference to appearing before a court shall be construed as including a reference to being brought before a court."

3–14 The time limit should wherever possible be complied with so as to avoid any unnecessary adjournment of proceedings. The time limit is however not absolute. A party can, with the leave of the court rely on such a defence notwithstanding a failure to comply with the time limits set out under section 21(5). Failure to meet the procedural requirements will therefore not necessarily be fatal to a defence on the merits. On application to the court, the court has an unfettered discretion to grant leave to any defaulting defendant to rely on the defence notwithstanding a failure to serve a statutory notice on the prosecutor at all or within the time limits imposed by the Act. It is however important that the time limits should be complied with so that the Food Authority/Prosecutor is informed as soon as possible that the real fault may lie with the third party.

The Food Authority/Prosecutor may on receipt of the notice reconsider the prosecution in the light of its contents. The Food Authority may consider it more appropriate to prosecute the third party identified in the notice. In such circumstances, the proceedings against the initial defendant may be withdrawn. In the event that the Food Authority/Prosecutor is served late with the statutory notice, then it is likely that the Food Authority/Prosecutor will require time to consider its contents and any further action. In these circumstances, any application for an adjournment of proceedings by the Prosecutor is likely to succeed.

By a parity of reasoning therefore, given that any injustice to the prosecution can be cured by an adjournment, it is submitted that seldom, if ever, would it be appropriate for a defence on the merits to be shut out on account of a procedural irregularity or failure to comply with the time limits for serving of the statutory notice provided by section 21(5) of the Act.

The construction of subsection (5) does however beg the question of **3–15** whether or not "another person" includes a person under the control of the defendant. It is clear from the case of *Tesco Supermarkets* v. *Nattrass*[3] that even persons of managerial status are not to be regarded synonymously with, for example, a defendant company. Therefore if the act or default of an employee employed by the defendant company results in a commission of an offence by the defendants company, the question arises as to whether or not the defendant company needs to serve a statutory notice in order to rely on the defence due diligence.

It is arguable that notice should be served in accordance with section 21 (5). It is submitted however that in such circumstances, no notice is required unless it is to be alleged that the responsible employee was acting outside the scope of his employment (*e.g.* malicious tampering with or contamination of food products or their labelling).

If the employee acts in the normal course of his employment so as to cause an offence to be committed by the defendant employer, then it is submitted that no notice is required because the wording of section 21(1) expressly includes reference to the avoidance of the commission of the

[3] [1972] A.C. 153, H.L.

offence by himself (the defendant) or "by a person under his control" as opposed to "another person" or third party.

The words "another person" are taken up later in subsections (3) and (4) and have been referred to earlier in section 20 of the Act. It is submitted that the distinction is deliberate.

3–16　The statutory defence under section 21 of the FSA differs, for example, from that provided under the Trade Descriptions Act 1968. The statutory defence under the 1968 Act required proof of two separate elements namely an "act or default of another person," *and* "all reasonable precautions and all due diligence" to avoid commission of the offence. Section 21 (1) of the FSA introduces a new concept with a general defence of due diligence requiring proof only that the person charged:

> "took all reasonable precautions and exercised all due diligence to avoid the commission of the offence *by himself or by a person under his control*" (italics added for emphasis).

The words "by himself or by a person under his control" are new to food law and introduce a new and conceptually different statutory defence to this food legislation. In the context of section 21 of the FSA it is clear that "a person under his control" includes all employees of the person charged. "Another person" therefore on a true construction of section 21 of the 1990 Act is not therefore intended to be an employee but rather a supplier, agent or other third party independent from the employment of the person charged.

Further, the purpose behind the requirement for notice is reflected in the wording of section 21(5) itself. The purpose behind the requirement for notice, it is submitted, is to assist the Food Authority/Prosecutor in the identification of any person responsible for the commission of the offence *other than the defendant* or a person acting under his control.

3–17　If the defendant company, for example, was responsible for *the commission* of the offence, then in order to rely successfully on the defence of due diligence under section 21 (1), he will need to establish a sufficient system for the avoidance of the commission of the offence which necessarily will include any act or default committed by a person or employee under the defendant company's control and working under the system.

If the system of work and organisation was inadequate to prevent the commission of the particular offence, then the fact that the act or omission was the responsibility of the employee or a person under control of the defendant company will be immaterial because the defendant company in those circumstances would not be able to escape liability. In practice it will be sensible even in the case of "employee fault" to serve a section 21(5)

Notice on the Prosecution/Enforcement Authority and to avoid any procedural dispute at trial.

Format of Statutory Notice

3–18

In cases where the defendant alleges that the offence was due to the fault of another person there is no longer any requirement upon the defendant to lay his own information in the Magistrate's Court against a person whom he alleges to be actually guilty of the offence. The only requirement is now to serve a Statutory Notice in accordance with section 21(5) of the Act. The Notice must be in writing. Otherwise there are no requirements as to the form of the Notice.

In all cases where service of a Notice is appropriate, the notice should to the extent of the defendant's information at the time be sufficient to assist the Enforcement Authority/Prosecutor in the identification of the "other person" (or persons) responsible.

Causal Connection Between Offence and Statutory Defence

3–19

It should be noted that the statutory defence under section 21(1) is specific in its terms of reference. Section 21(1) reads:

> "**21.**— (1) In any proceedings *for an offence* . . . it shall . . . be a defence for the person charged to prove that he took all reasonable precautions and exercised all due diligence to avoid the commission *of the offence* by himself or by a person under his control" (italics added for emphasis).

A similar form of words is uniformly reflected in each of the subsections dealing with the statutory defences under both sections 21 and the separate statutory defence under section 22.[4] This is important particularly in the context of criminal proceedings. It will only be necessary for the defendant to prove that the relevant part or parts of his system of operation were to the statutorily required standard to avoid the particular offence or offences charged. The defendant will not therefore be required to demonstrate that his entire system of operation was, in every aspect to the required statutory standard. Only that part or parts of his operation which could properly be

---

[4] See *post*, para. 3–20.

considered relevant to the commission of the particular offence will be material in the proceedings.

Likewise, it will not or very rarely will it be open to the Prosecution/Enforcement Authority to introduce evidence of deficient procedures or practices in the defendant's system of operation if there is no causal connection between such deficiencies or practices and the commission of the particular offence or offences alleged. Such evidence would either be inadmissible or likely to be prejudicial and excluded under section 78 of the Police and Criminal Evidence Act 1984.

The appropriate method of dealing with observed deficiencies in procedures or practices in a system of operation within a food business which have not resulted in a commission of any offence that may potentially do so and hence require improvement is by way of an issue of a statutory Improvement Notice under section 10 of the FSA. If the Improvement Notice is not successfully appealed under section 37 of the Act and is not complied with then an offence is committed and the criminal sanction takes effect.

3–20 ## Statutory Defence of Publication in the Course of Business (*section 22*)

Section 22 of the FSA provides a specific defence to an offence under section 15 of the Act for falsely describing or presenting food whether by display, labelling or advertising. Section 15 is designed to guard against the risk that food may be so described, displayed, labelled or advertised in order to mislead the consumer as to the nature, substance or quality of the food. Section 22 states that:

"In proceedings for an offence under any of the preceding provisions of this Part consisting of the advertisement for sale of any food, it shall be a defence for the person charged to prove:
(a) that he is a person whose business it is to publish or arrange for the publication of advertisements; and
(b) that he received the advertisement in the ordinary course of business and did not know and had no reason to suspect that its publication would amount to an offence under that provision.

Thus section 22 protects the person who unwittingly offends the provisions of section 15 in the course of a publication or advertisement business.

There are two essential ingredients which need to be established if this defence is to be relied upon. First, it must be proved under section 22(a) that the defendant is in the business of publishing or advertising. Secondly, under section 22(b) the defendant must prove that he received the advertisement in the ordinary course of business and acted innocently.

Similarly to section 21(3)(c) but in contrast to section 21(4)(c) the defendant is not vested with constructive knowledge and is therefore under no positive duty to scrutinise or check the accuracy of the advertisement independently. Again, in the circumstances where a person publishes an advertisement in the bona fide course of his business which in fact is a misleading advertisement an offence will be committed.

The offender will not be liable if the statutory defence under section 22 is established by him on the balance of probabilities. In such circumstances the Enforcement Authority will be able to prosecute the third party culprit responsible for the section 15 offence by virtue of section 20 of the FSA.

Best Practice   3–21

The best run food business may on occasion commit an offence under the FSA. Rogue or deliberate contamination of food, mechanical malfunction and human error can never by wholly eliminated whatever system is operated. In such an event the FSA places a burden on all persons operating business to take all reasonable precautions and exercise all due diligence to prevent such offences.

Once the offence itself is established the burden of proof rests on the operator of the food business to establish the statutory defence relied on. It is therefore not enough that all reasonable precautions are taken and all due diligence was exercised: the defendant or operator of a food business must be able to establish the defence *ex post facto* in accordance with proceedings to the civil standard of proof.

In the light of the FSA and the severe penalties and sanctions that may be imposed following conviction it is sensible and appropriate for all persons likely to be affected by the provisions of the FSA to set in place a verifiable system of operation which serves to secure compliance with the legislation. Listed below are a number of features which may be included in a framework of Best Practice.

Features of Best Practice   3–22

    (a) Competent and trained staff;
    (b) Records or documentation relating to the training or instruction of staff;

(c) Appropriate levels of supervision and inspection by senior members of staff or external bodies;

(d) Records or documentation of a system of supervision or inspection;

(e) Oral or written confirmation of supervision and inspection conducted on a random or a spot-check basis in addition to any regular routine and inspection;

(f) A system of sample testing;

(g) Records or documentation verifying the system of sample testing;

(h) Random destructive sample testing, if appropriate;

(i) A system of recording complaints, faults and deficiencies in equipment or machinery;

(j) A system of fault/defect correction;

(k) Records or documentation verification that faults and defects are corrected and remedied properly;

(l) Provision of appropriate, efficient and well-maintained machinery and equipment;

(m) Regular service and maintenance of all machinery and equipment;

(n) Records or documentation relating to the service or maintenance of essential machinery and equipment;

(o) Oral confirmation of satisfactory standards of hygiene, housekeeping and cleanliness.

The features listed above are not necessarily exhaustive. Nor are the features listed above measures which it would be reasonable to adopt in all instances. To comply with all such practices would be to conform to the best possible practice. In many instances it will neither be practical nor reasonable to institute and maintain such rigorous measures. Different considerations will apply to different food businesses and all circumstances should be taken into account in consideration of each particular case. The surest way of achieving an acceptable system of operation, particularly in areas of doubt, would be to consult or seek guidance and advice from the local Food Authority.

3–23 Risk Assessment

Risk assessment would seem to be the crux of any due diligence defence. The concept of risk assessment is one which has found favour in community legislation elsewhere, particularly in the field of health and safety legislation.

A new European Union food hygiene directive (93/43/EEC) has recently been implemented and will require that the current Food Hygiene (General) Regulations 1970 be revised to take account of the contents of that directive. The general requirements of the Directive which will eventually be incorporated into UK legislation are useful to set out, as certain aspects of the directive have an impact upon any potential due diligence defence.

The directive contains provisions to require that:

(a) preparation, processing, manufacturing, packaging, storing, transportation, handling and offering for sale or supply of food stuffs is dealt with in a hygienic manner;

(b) the rules of hygiene set out in a schedule to the directive should be complied with. (This schedule lays down requirements for food businesses of various types);

(c) food handlers should be trained in relevant aspects of food hygiene;

(d) food businesses should identify and control potential food hazards;

(e) food authorities should give "due consideration" to voluntary industry guides on good hygiene practice.

It is expected that the general principles of HACCP (Hazard Analysis and Critical Control Point) will be adopted by food businesses in complying with the directive and the regulations when they are eventually brought into force, in order that appropriate risk assessments are carried out.

Chapter 4
Administrative Provisions

CROWN PREMISES 4–01

General

As a general rule, the Crown is not normally subject to statute law. The FSA section 54(1) makes the Crown expressly subject to the Act and all orders and regulations made under it.

However, section 54(2) provides that no provision of the FSA can make the Crown criminally liable in respect of any contravention of the FSA. The High Court is given power to declare unlawful any act or omission of the Crown upon the application of an Enforcement Authority. By normal custom, the Crown will abide by any such declaration.

Individual employees are *not* accorded the immunity from criminal liability, and section 54(3) ensures that all provisions of the FSA and orders and regulations made thereunder will apply to individuals despite the effects of section 54(2) in relation to the Crown itself.

The person of the Sovereign (which by section 38(3) of the Crown proceedings Act 1947 includes the Prince of Wales in his capacity as Duke of Cornwall and Lancaster) is not affected by any provision of the FSA.[1] The net effect of section 54 is to ensure that:

---

[1] See s. 54(5).

1. The normal regulatory provisions of the FSA—powers to issue Improvement Notices, Prohibition Notices, etc., will apply to Crown premises,
2. The Crown cannot be made criminally liable for any breaches of the FSA including failure to comply with improvement notices, etc.;
3. A declaration can issue from the High Court to confirm that any act/omission of the Crown is unlawful;
4. Any person employed in the public service of the Crown has no immunity from criminal liability in relation to the FSA.

4–02 Entry to Crown Premises

Certain types of Crown premises may require that access to those premises be restricted for reasons of national security. Accordingly, section 54(4) provides that the Secretary of State may issue a National Security Certificate on the basis that it is expedient in the interests of national security that the powers of entry contained in section 32 of the FSA should *not* be exercisable in relation to certain premises.

4–03 The Code of Practice

A Code of Practice on enforcement of the FSA in relation to Crown premises has been issued under section 40 of the FSA. The Code deals at some length with the question of entry to Crown premises and the related issues of inspections and enforcement provisions.

To enable authorised officers to decide how best to deal with Crown premises, the Code suggests a three tier categorisation:

> *Group 1*— Premises with no security problems, *e.g.* restaurants in Royal Parks.
> *Group 2*— Premises with restricted entry but only a slight security risk, *e.g.* most government buildings.
> *Group 3*— Premises with a high degree of security, *e.g.* military installations, royal residences.

The Code recommends that any inspections of Group 3 premises should be preceded by notification to the person responsible for those premises of the proposal to make the inspection. A similar recommendation exists in relation to the first visit which would be made to Group 2 premises.

Authorised Officers are specifically advised in the Code of Practice that any restriction on the timing of proposed visits to Group 3 premises are *not* to be regarded as an obstruction for the purposes of an offence under section 33(1)(a) of the FSA.

Any such purported restriction in relation to any other type of premises, whether Crown premises or not, would certainly give grounds for proceedings under section 33(1)(a) of the FSA.

Enforcement

4–04

The FSA provides that the Crown cannot be criminally liable for breaches of the Act or Regulations/Orders made under it. The Code of Practice however, reminds Authorised Officers that very often, the persons responsible for catering on Crown premises may be contract caterers operating as private companies. The criminal liability for such companies is unaffected by the fact that they operate on Crown premises.

The crucial issue is to consider whose act or omission has led to the breach of the FSA. The Code of Practice mistakenly suggests that it is not open to a Magistrates Court to issue a Prohibition Order in relation to Crown premises, because such an Order can only follow a conviction under Food Hygiene[2] or Processing Regulations.

It is submitted that this advice is incorrect. Section 11 of the FSA[3] which deals with Prohibition Orders provides that the appropriate prohibition may be imposed following conviction of "the proprietor of a food business." Such a proprietor may be a privately contracted caterer, operating on Crown premises rather than the Crown itself. Therefore it would seem that the Magistrates Court would have the appropriate power.

SAMPLING AND ANALYSIS

4–05

In very many cases, particularly relating to offences under sections 7, 8 or 14 of the FSA, a successful prosecution may depend on food samples being correctly taken and properly analysed.

Sections 29, 30 and 31 of the FSA relate respectively to provisions in respect of the procurement of samples, the analysis or examination of such samples, and regulations to deal with the relevant procedures followed.

---

[2] S.I. 1970 No. 1172 as amended by S.I. 1990 No. 1431 and S.I. 1991 No. 1343.
[3] See *ante*, para. 1–37.

4–06 Procurement of samples

Authorised Officers of Enforcement Authorities are given specific powers to purchase or take samples of food or contact materials by section 29 of the FSA.

It should be remembered that the "Enforcement Authority" for any particular area will not always be the same as the "Food Authority". This is because the functions of an Enforcement Authority may be exercised by other bodies *e.g.* the Ministers by virtue of section 6(3) and 6(4) of the FSA.

Section 29 allows an officer to:

"(a) purchase a sample of any food, or any substance capable of being used in the preparation of food;

(b) take a sample of any food, or any such substance which—
  (i) appears to him to be intended for sale, or to have been sold, for human consumption; or
  (ii) is found by him on or in any premises which he is authorised to enter by or under section 32 below;

(c) take a sample from any food source, or a sample of any contact material, which is found by him on or in any such premises;

(d) take a sample of any article or substance which is found by him on or in any such premises and which he has reason to believe may be required as evidence in proceedings under any part of this Act or of regulations or orders made under it."

4–07 Procedure for obtaining samples

The Code of Practice on sampling for analysis or examination[4] requires that the samples should be taken by officers who are "properly trained in the appropriate techniques." It may be that if samples are taken by officers who are not so trained the samples may be inadmissible as evidence in subsequent proceedings.

Section 31 of the FSA makes provision for regulations to be made to deal with the detailed manner in which samples should be obtained. Regulations have been made under section 31 in the form of the Food Safety (Sampling and Qualifications) Regulations 1990.[5]

Regulation 6 of the Regulations sets out three different ways for dealing with samples *for analysis*:

---

[4] Code of Practice No. 7.
[5] S.I. 1990 No. 2463.

(a) Regulation 6(1)—a sample should be divided into three parts-
—put each part into sealed container—mark each container—give
one to the owner of the sample and give him notice that it will be
analysed. Send one for analysis—retain one sample.

(b) Regulation 6(2)—Where the sample consists of a sealed container,
e.g. tin cans, and opening them might impede a proper analysis,
the officer may divide the containers into three lots and treat each
lot as a separate part and carry out the same procedure as in (a)
above.

(c) Regulation 6(4)—Where the sample cannot be divided into parts,
the sample should be submitted for analysis and the owner given
notice accordingly.

The purpose of retaining a third sample is to enable it to be submitted for **4–08**
analysis by the Government Chemists if a court so orders or if the
Authorised Officer and the owner agree.[6]

Regulation 8 covers the procedure for dealing with a sample for *examination*. This procedure requires simply that the sample be placed in a marked
sealed container and submitted for examination having given notice of the
examination to the owner. It is vitally important to a successful prosecution
that all of the procedural aspects of taking and analysing a sample are
strictly followed. It is well established by case law that any failure to follow
the requirements must result in an acquittal.

In *Skeate* v. *Moore*[7] an Authorised Officer took a sample of six meat pies
from a baker. The pies were divided into three lots of two, and two of the
pies were sent for analysis. The baker was prosecuted for selling a meat pie
which failed to comply with regulations controlling the meat content for
certain products. The Court of Appeal quashed the baker's conviction as
there could not be a prosecution relating to *one* meat pie when a number of
pies had been taken as the statutory sample.

The importance of strictly following statutory requirements relating to
sampling was emphasised in a case involving the sampling provisions under
the Water Resources Act 1991—the *National Rivers Authority* v. *Harcros
Timber & Building Supplies Ltd*[8]. In that case, a sample of water/effluent
which had not been taken in accordance with the statutory provisions was
held to be inadmissible in evidence as one part of the sample had not been
given to the defendant company.

---

[6] *Ibid.*, reg. 7.
[7] [1972] 1 W.L.R. 110.
[8] (1992) 156 J.P. 743; (1992) 156 J.P.N. 588.

4–09 Submission of samples for analysis/examination

The FSA draws a distinction between "Analysis" of a sample and "Examination" of a sample. "Analysis" is defined in section 53(1) of the FSA to *include* a microbiological assay and any technique for establishing the composition of food. "Examination" is defined in section 28(2) of the FSA simply as a microbiological examination.

Once the sample has been properly obtained, the officer must consider whether it should be submitted for analysis or examination. If submitted for analysis, the sample must be submitted either to the public analyst for the area where the sample was obtained or the public analyst for the area which includes the area for the Food Authority. If submitted for examination, the sample should be submitted to a food examiner. A food examiner is by virtue of section 30(9) of the FSA defined as a person who conforms with the requirements set out in regulation 4 of the Food Safety (Sampling and Qualifications) Regulations 1990.[9]

4–10   A sample may also be submitted for analysis/examination by any person who has purchased the food under section 30(2) of the FSA.

This provision enables a disgruntled member of the public to submit a suspect sample direct for analysis/examination without recourse to the Enforcement Authority. If there is no public analyst for any particular area, section 30(4) of the FSA provides that a sample for analysis may be submitted to any other public analyst. The examiner/analyst to whom a sample is submitted has a statutory duty to deal with the sample as soon as practicable.[10]

He is allowed, however, to demand in advance payment of a reasonable fee where a sample is submitted by a person who is not an Authorised Officer or the analyst is not the public analyst of the area in question.

Once the analysis/examination has been completed the public analyst/food examiner must sign a certificate specifying the result of the test and give the signed certificate to the person who submitted the sample to him.

4–11   Any such certificate, properly signed is made admissible in Court proceedings by section 30(8) of the FSA without the need for any further requirement such as statement made under the Criminal Justice Act 1967 to produce the certificate. The certificate cannot be used in evidence where the other party to the proceedings requires that the person who signed the certificate should be called as a witness.[11]

[9] S.I. 1990 No. 2463.
[10] FSA, s. 30(5).
[11] FSA, s. 30(8).

A form of certificate is prescribed in the appropriate regulations which also provide that the owner of the sample shall be entitled to be supplied with a copy of the certificate upon request.

FORM OF DOCUMENTS   4–12

Section 49 of the FSA provides that certain matters must be put into writing, *i.e*:

(a) all documents authorised or required by this Act to be given, made or issued by a food authority; and

(b) all notices and applications authorised or required by or under this Act to be given or made to, or to any officer of, such an authority.

Certain documents are authorised to be used in a prescribed form, *e.g.* the form to register food business premises with a Food Authority, or a certificate of analysis of a food sample.

Documents which a Food Authority are required or authorised to make under the FSA may be signed by the appropriate officer of the authority. Such an officer may be either the officer within whose sphere of responsibility the document falls, or any officer specifically authorised in writing by the authority to sign those documents.

Any document which purports to bear the signature of an appropriate officer is deemed to have been made or issued by the Food Authority unless the contrary can be proven. For the purposes of these documents, a "signature" is defined as including a facsimile of a signature howsoever reproduced.

SERVICE OF DOCUMENTS   4–13

The FSA 1990 makes provision throughout the Act for the service of various documents on certain persons. For the avoidance of any doubt, section 50 of the FSA makes provision as to how documents should be served, if no other specific provision is made. A number of options are available. Documents may be served either:

(i) by delivering to that person;

(ii) in the case of an authorised officer, by leaving it or sending it in a prepaid letter addressed to him at his office;

    (iii) in the case of a body corporate, by delivery at the registered or principal office or sending it in a prepaid letter to that address;

    (iv) in the case of any other person by leaving it or sending it in a prepaid letter at his usual or last known address.

In certain circumstances, documents may have to be served on the owner or occupier of premises, where it proves impossible to determine the identity or address of that person. In such a case, the relevant document may be served by addressing it to the "owner" or "occupier" of the named premises and by:

    (a) delivering it to someone on the premises or;

    (b) affixing it or a copy of it to a conspicuous part of the premises if there is no one on the premises.

Chapter 5
Food Safety Law—The European Dimension

INTRODUCTION

No work on English food safety law, however practically orientated, would be complete without some discussion of the impact of E.U. law. Since the subject is enormous, and the space available limited, any such discussion must by necessity, be confined within very narrow parameters. For a comprehensive introduction to Community law generally, see Kapteyn and VerLoren van Themaats' *Introduction to the Law of the European Communities*:[1] For a comprehensive review of E.U. food measures, see *Butterworths Law of Food and Drugs*.[2]

The European Community is an economic community founded, *inter alia*, upon the principle of the free movements of commodities within its boundaries. In one sense, food is simply a commodity to be traded around the Community, like any other. Yet, because of the dangers posed to human health by contaminated or substandard food, the food trade in developed countries tends to be more closely regulated than other forms of commercial activity. The nature and degree of that regulation will naturally vary from country to country. A nation's gastronomy is an essential aspect

---

[1] (2nd Ed.), Kluwer 1989.
[2] Painter, Butterworths 1992.

93

of its culture. Contrasting attitudes to food safety may thus be seen as a vivid aspect of the cultural diversity of nations, even those as closely linked as the Member States of the E.U. The recent listeria scare served to emphasise the difference between public attitudes in France, and those in Britain, to the use of unpasteurised milk in cheese-making. It can therefore, readily be seen that in a community founded upon a principle of the free circulation of goods between Member States, the application of different national rules and standards relating to food safety could lead to discriminatory practices, threatening the establishment of a free market in food products. In fact, the jurisprudence of the European Court of Justice effectively established a single Community market in food products several years ago, as will be seen when the *Cassis de Dijon*[3] case is discussed.

5–02 ## SOME GENERAL PRINCIPLES OF COMMUNITY LAW

Before the impact of Community action on food safety can be properly appreciated, certain fundamental principles relating to the interaction of the Community legal order with that of its Member States must be considered. It is essential to understand that the Community represents a wholly new legal order in international law, whereby those Member States have agreed to limit their sovereign rights within the spheres of operation of the Community. Thus, independently of the legislation of Member States, Community law not only imposes obligations on individuals, but also confers on them rights, which they can invoke and enforce before the national courts of Member States.

Community law is derived from four basic sources:

1. The E.U. Treaty and Protocols, as amended by subsequent Treaties, the most recent of which being the Single European Act of 1986;
2. Secondary legislation of the E.U. Institutions, *i.e.* Regulations, Directives and Decisions;
3. The Jurisprudence of the European Court of Justice (and of the Courts of Justice of the ECSC and Euratom before the merger of the Communities in 1965);

---

[3] 120/78, *Rewe-Zentral* AG v. *Bundesmonopolverwalting für Branntwein*: [1979] E.C.R. 649, [1979] 3 C.M.L.R. 494.

4. Treaties entered into by E.U. institutions on behalf of the Community.

Treaty Law

5–03

 The primary source of E.U. Law is, naturally, to be found in the Treaty of Rome as amended. It is a characteristic of that Treaty, that its objectives are expressed in broad terms. Its Articles may be said to be the foundations upon which the edifice of Community Law has been built. The formulation of detailed rules of law has been the task of the legislative and judicial institutions of the Communities. Thus, over the years, a vast body of secondary legislation and case law has evolved.

EC Secondary Legislation

5–04

Article 189 of the Treaty of Rome provides that:

> "In order to carry out their task, the Council and the Commission shall, in accordance with the provisions of this Treaty, make regulations, issue directives, take decisions, make recommendations or deliver opinions.
> A regulation shall have general application. It shall be binding in its entirety and directly applicable in all Member States.
> A directive shall be binding as to the result to be achieved on each Member State to which it is addressed, but shall leave to the national authorities, the choice of the form and methods.
> A decision shall be binding in its entirety upon those to whom it is addressed.
> Recommendations and opinions have no binding force."

 The structure of Community secondary legislation is thus essentially, hierarchical. A regulation comprises rules of general application, binding in all Member States without the need for the national authorities to do anything further by way of implementing legislation. Directives, on the other hand, although binding as to the objective to be achieved, vest Member States with complete discretion as to the juridical vehicle to be employed at national level. Decisions are by their very nature, of limited import. They may be addressed to individuals or Member States.

 Of the three types of secondary legislation described above, historically, the directive was the most commonly used vehicle for implementing the Community's food safety policy. The poor response of some Member

States in translating directives into effective national legislation, has given rise to an increasing tendency to use the regulation as the juridical vehicle of choice.

5–05 Direct Effect

Community Law, in all its forms, does not merely create rights and obligations enforceable as between Member States. It is also capable of creating rights (and obligations) which individuals may invoke before national courts, in the context of their legal relations either with Member States or other individuals.

The tendency of a provision of Community law to confer rights and duties upon individuals, (as opposed to Member States), which those individuals can enforce before national courts, is known as *direct effect*. The tendency of a provision to create rights enforceable by an individual against a Member State is known as *vertical direct effect*. Whether a provision has this effect is a question of interpretation.

The ground rules for establishing whether a provision is directly effective were established by the European Court of Justice as far back as 1963, in the landmark Case of 26/62, *Van Gend en Loos* v. *Nederlandse Belastingad-ministratie*.[4] That case concerned Article 12 of the Treaty of Rome, which prohibits Member States from introducing between themselves any new customs duties on imports or charges having equivalent effect or from raising any existing duties. This provision obviously went to the very root of the establishment of the Common Market for goods envisaged by the Treaty. The case was referred to the European Court of Justice by the Dutch Tariefcommissie for a ruling under Article 177 of the Treaty on the question whether Article 12 gave rise to rights which nationals of Member States were entitled to enforce before national courts.

5–06   The European Court of Justice answered this question in the affirmative. The wording of Article 12 contained a clear and unconditional prohibition amounting to a negative obligation. That obligation was not qualified by any reservation on the part of States which would make its implementation conditional upon any positive legislative measure enacted under national law:

---

[4] 26/62, *NV Algemene Transport–en Expeditie Onderneming Van Gend en Loos* v. *Nederlandse Belastingadministratie*: [1963] E.C.R. 1, [1963] C.M.L.R. 105.

"The very nature of the prohibition makes it ideally adapted to produce direct effects in the legal relationship between Member States and their subjects".[5]

The principles enunciated in this case have been refined and developed by the Court in its subsequent jurisprudence. In order to satisfy the requirements for direct effect, the provision in question must:

1. be sufficiently clear and precise;
2. establish an unconditional obligation;
3. be completely and legally perfect requiring no subsequent measures to be taken by community institutions or Member States with discretionary power in the matter.

A regulation is, by its very nature, liable to be productive of a direct effect. However, the mere fact that an instrument is published as a regulation in the Official Journal of the European Communities, does not automatically imbue it with the attribute of being directly effective. Whether it is possessed of the three characteristics essential to give rise to a direct effect, is a question of interpretation where the substance, rather than the form in which that instrument is expressed will be the determining factor. It may be that within an instrument published as a regulation, there are provisions which lack sufficient clarity, fail to impose unconditional obligations or leave essential matters to the discretion of Member States. Such provisions, whatever the title of the legal instrument in which they are embodied, will not be held to have direct effect.

In contrast to regulations, directives are not expressed by Article 189, to   **5–07** be "directly applicable". Indeed, the fact that the means of implementation is left to the discretion of Member States, tends to suggest that directives are not designed to produce directly effective rules. In reality, the European Court of Justice has held that provided a directive possesses the necessary three characteristics, there is no reason why its provisions cannot have direct effect. In view of the Community's preference for the directive as the primary vehicle for the implementation of its environmental policy[1] it is important to examine the circumstances in which they may be held to have direct effect in a little detail.

In Case 9/70, *Franz Grad* v. *Finanzamt Traustein*[6], the Court stated that the mere fact that under Article 189, only regulations were expressed to be directly applicable did not preclude other legal measures referred to therein

---

[5] 26/62: [1963] E.C.R. 1 at p. 13, [1963] C.M.L.R. 105.
[6] 9/70, *Franz Grad* v. *Finanzamt Traustein*: [1970] E.C.R. 825, [1971] C.M.L.R. 1.

from producing similar effects. To hold otherwise might undermine the useful effect (*effet utile*) of such measures, and render them impotent.

5–08   The principles set out in *Grad* [7] were followed and refined by the Court in Case 41/74, *Van Duyn* v. *Home Office*. [8] Miss Van Duyn was a Dutch National who wished to enter the United Kingdom in order to take up employment as a Secretary with the Church of Scientology at East Grinstead. The Home Office refused her leave to enter the country on public policy grounds, based on the fact that it considered the activities of the Church to be socially harmful. She brought an action against the Home Office in the High Court in England. The High Court referred certain questions to the European Court of Justice under Article 177. One of the questions required the Court to consider whether a directive concerning the free movement of persons within the Community was a measure upon which individuals could rely. Advocate General Mayras, in his opinion, reiterated the criteria for direct effect originally proposed by Advocate General Gand in Case 48/65 *Luticke*, [9] which had been adopted by the European Court of Justice in subsequent cases, as follows:

> " . . . the provision must impose a clear and precise obligation on Member States; it must be unconditional, in other words subject to no limitation; if, however, a provision is subject to certain limitations, their nature and extent must be exactly defined; finally, the implementation of a Community rule must not be subject to the adoption of any subsequent rules or regulations on the part either of Community institutions or of the Member States, so that, in particular, Member States must not be left any real discretion with regard to the application of the rule in question".

M. Mayras went on to say that:

> "When faced with a directive, it is therefore necessary to examine, in each case, whether the wording, nature and general scheme of the provisions in question are capable of producing direct effects between the Member States to whom the directive is addressed and their subjects".

5–09   The mere fact that Member States were given the choice of form and method of implementation which accord with their national law did not

---

[7] *Ibid.*
[8] 41/74, *Van Duyn* v. *Home Office*: [1975] Ch. 358.
[9] 48/65, *Alfons Lütticke GmbH* v. *EEC Commission*: [1966] E.C.R. 19, [1966] C.M.L.R. 378.

imply that a directive could not be directly effective. The Court adopted the same approach. It stated that:

> "In particular, where the Community authorities have, by directive, imposed on Member States the obligation to pursue a particular course of conduct, the useful effect of such an act would be weakened if individuals were prevented from relying on it before their national courts and if the latter were prevented from taking it into consideration as an element of Community Law".

The Supremacy of EC Law   5–10

Directly effective provisions of Community Law, if invoked by individuals before the Courts of Member States may provoke a conflict between the domestic legal order and that of the Community. In such a case which law takes precedence? No guidance is provided by the Treaty.

The European Court of Justice has, however, made it clear that Community Law takes precedence over all national laws, whatever their nature, no matter how deeply rooted they may be in the constitution of a Member State.[10]

In Case 106/77 *Amministrazione delle Finanze dello Stato SpA* v. *Simmenthal SpA*,[11] the European Court of Justice held that to give legal effect to a national legislative measure which as incompatible with Community Law would be to deny the effectiveness of the obligations freely entered into by Member States, would strike at the very foundations of the Community. The Court went on to say:[12]

> "every national court must, in a case within its jurisdiction apply Community Law in its entirety and protect rights which the latter confers on individuals and must accordingly set aside any provision of national law which may conflict with it, whether prior or subsequent to the Community rule".

Precisely how effect is given to the principle of the primacy of Community Law is a question for the courts of each Member State. In the United Kingdom, the courts have used two different avenues, which in practice have had the effect of according primacy to Community Law. Thus,

---

[10] 11/70, *Internationale Handelsgesellschaft mbH* v. *Einfuhr—und Vorratsstelle für Getreide und Futtermittel*: [1970] E.C.R. 1125; [1972] C.M.L.R. 255.
[11] 106/77, *Amministrazione delle Finanze dello Stato SpA* v. *Simmenthal SpA*: [1978] E.C.R. 629, [1978] 3 C.M.L.R. 263.
[12] *Ibid.*, at p. 644.

although there is uniformity in the judicial approach to the end result, finding consistency in the means by which that end has been achieved, is difficult.

5–11 Community Action on Food Safety

The impact of Community initiatives on food safety law has been considerable, with the European Commission adopting a highly interventionist position. Thus, there has been a steady movement towards the harmonisation of food law within the Community over a number of years and an ever increasing flow of measures emanating from Brussels. Community action on the use of colouring and preservatives in food, for example, dates back to the early 1960s. The compliance record of the United Kingdom, in promulgating laws to implement Community measures has been good. The Food Safety Act 1990 is broadly compatible with E.U. law and has, built into its scheme, a mechanism for ensuring that United Kingdom Law is kept apace with developments in E.U. food law. Accordingly, section 17(2) of the FSA provides that:

> "(2) As respects any directly applicable Community provision which relates to food, food sources or contact materials and for which, in their opinion, it is appropriate to provide under this Act, the Ministers may by regulations—
>   (a) make such provision as they consider necessary or expedient for the purpose of securing that the Community provision is administered, executed and enforced under this Act; and
>   (b) apply such of the provisions of this Act as may be specified in the regulations in relation to the Community provision with such modifications, if any, as may be so specified."

The effect of this provision is to vest a rule-making power in Ministers, enabling them to rapidly implement Community Provisions, without the need for legislation to be passed by Parliament.

5–12 The Role of the European Court of Justice—"Cassis de Dijon"

It has been stated earlier that one of the founding principles of the Community. is that of the free movement of goods between Member States. Thus, Title 1 of the Treaty of Rome reads "Free Movement of Goods". Chapter 2 of that Title deals with the elimination of quantitative restrictions (quotas) between Member States. Article 30 of the Treaty states:

> "Quantitative restrictions on imports and all measures having equivalent effect shall, without prejudice to the following provisions, be prohibited between Member States."

Quantitative restrictions are measures which amount to a total or partial restriction on imports, exports or goods in transit. A working definition of measures having equivalent effect was provided by the European Court of Justice in Case 8/74, *Procureur du Roi* v. *Dassonville*.[13] Under this definition,

> "All trading rules enacted by Member States which are capable of hindering directly or indirectly, actually or potentially, intra-community trade are to be considered as measures having an effect equivalent to quantitative restrictions."

In the landmark Case 120/78 *Rewe-Zentral AG* v. *Bundesmonopolverwaltung für Branntwein*,[14] *"Cassis de Dijon"*, the European Court of Justice went a long way towards creating a free market in food products within the Community. In that Case, German law prescribed a minimum alcohol content of 25 per cent. for certain liquors, among them cassis, an ingredient in the making of the drink, kir. German produced cassis had the requisite alcohol content. The effect of the law was to preclude the marketing of French cassis, which contained a maximum of 20 per cent. alcohol, in Germany. It was held that the German law infringed Article 30 of the Treaty. This was an example of a product in free circulation in one Member State, France, being discriminated against in another, Germany. The Court enunciated the general rule that any product lawfully produced in one Member State must, in principle, be admitted to the market of any other Member State. The Court went on to state that obstacles to movement within the Community would only be permitted to the extent that they were necessary in order to satisfy *mandatory requirements* of the Community relating, *inter alia*, to the protection of public health and the defence of the consumer. Derogations from the general principle resulting from differences between commercial and technical rules between Member States will only be acceptable to the extent that the rules:

---

[13] 8/74, *Procureur du Roi* v. *Dassonville*: [1974] E.C.R. 837, [1974] 2 C.M.L.R. 436.
[14] 120/78, *Rewe-Zentral AG* v. *Bundesmonopolverwaltung für Branntwein*: [1979] E.C.R. 649; [1979] 3 C.M.L.R. 494.

    (i) are necessary, that is appropriate and not excessive to satisfy mandatory requirements, *i.e.* public health, protection of consumers or the environment, the fairness of commercial transactions, etc.,

    (ii) serve a purpose in the general interest which is compelling enough to justify an exception to a fundamental rule of the Treaty, such as the free movement of goods;

    (iii) are essential for such a purpose to be obtained, *i.e.* are the means which are the most appropriate and at the same time least hinder trade.

5–13   The decision prompted the Commission to communicate guidelines regarding the position which the Community would adopt when faced with potentially discriminatory technical or qualitative trading rules.[15] The Commission indicated that it was concerned in particular with rules that govern the composition, designation, presentation and packaging of products, as well as rules requiring compliance with certain technical standards. Where a product "suitably and satisfactorily" fulfils the legitimate requirements of an exporting Member State's own rules as to public health, consumer protection, etc., the Member State into which the product is imported cannot justify a prohibition on the marketing of that product in its territory by claiming that the methods by which the former State fulfils those legitimate requirements is different from its own methods in relation to domestic products. The Commission has taken the view that an absolute prohibition on the marketing of a product in this way could never be considered necessary to satisfy a mandatory requirement. In any case the burden will lie on the national authority seeking to assert that its rules and regulations are necessary to satisfy the Community's mandatory requirements.

    It can readily be seen that this is an important decision in so far as it affects food in free circulation in the Community. It may be invoked, in appropriate circumstances, as a defence to a criminal charge. Its significance will naturally diminish as the movement towards total harmonisation of food law within the E.U. is completed.

---

[15] [1980] O.J. C256/2.

Appendix

Part 1—Food Safety Act 1990

Part 2—Code of Practice No. 6 (Schedule)

Appendix
Part 1

Food Safety Act 1990

CHAPTER 16

ARRANGEMENT OF SECTIONS

PART I

PRELIMINARY

PART II

MAIN PROVISIONS

Food safety

Consumer protection

105

Regulations

16. Food safety and consumer protection.
17. Enforcement of Community provisions.
18. Special provisions for particular food etc.
19. Registration and licensing of food premises.

Defences etc.

20. Offences due to fault of another person.
21. Defence of due diligence.
22. Defence of publication in the course of business.

Miscellaneous and supplemental

23. Provision of food hygiene training.
24. Provision of facilities for cleansing shellfish.
25. Orders for facilitating the exercise of functions.
26. Regulations and orders: supplementary provisions.

PART III

ADMINISTRATION AND ENFORCEMENT

Administration

27. Appointment of public analysts.
28. Provision of facilities for examinations.

Sampling and analysis etc.

29. Procurement of samples.
30. Analysis etc. of samples.
31. Regulation of sampling and analysis etc.

Powers of entry and obstruction etc.

32. Powers of entry.
33. Obstruction etc. of officers.

Offences

34. Time limit for prosecutions.
35. Punishment of offences.
36. Offences by bodies corporate.

107

59. Amendments, transitional provisions, savings and repeals.
60. Short title, commencement and extent.

SCHEDULES:

Food Safety Act 1990

1990 CHAPTER 16

An Act to make new provision in place of the Food Act 1984 (except Parts III and V), the Food and Drugs (Scotland) Act 1956 and certain other enactments relating to food; to amend Parts III and V of the said Act of 1984 and Part I of the Food and Environment Protection Act 1985; and for connected purposes. **6–01**

[29th June 1990]

Be it enacted by the Queen's most Excellent Majesty, by and with the advice and consent of the Lords Spiritual and Temporal, and Commons, in this present Parliament assembled, and by the authority of the same, as follows:—

PART I

PRELIMINARY

1.—(1) In this Act "food" includes— **6–02**

(a) drink;
(b) articles and substances of no nutritional value which are used for human consumption;
(c) chewing gum and other products of a like nature and use; and
(d) articles and substances used as ingredients in the preparation of food or anything falling within this subsection.

(2) In this Act "food" does not include—

    (a) live animals or birds, or live fish which are not used for human consumption while they are alive;

    (b) fodder or feeding stuffs for animals, birds or fish;

    (c) controlled drugs within the meaning of the Misuse of Drugs Act 1971; or

    (d) subject to such exceptions as may be specified in an order made by the Ministers—

        (i) medicinal products within the meaning of the Medicines Act 1968 in respect of which product licences within the meaning of that Act are for the time being in force; or

        (ii) other articles or substances in respect of which such licences are for the time being in force in pursuance of orders under section 104 or 105 of that Act (application of Act to other articles and substances).

(3) In this Act, unless the context otherwise requires—

"business" includes the undertaking of a canteen, club, school, hospital or institution, whether carried on for profit or not, and any undertaking or activity carried on by a public or local authority;

"commercial operation", in relation to any food or contact material, means any of the following, namely—

    (a) selling, possessing for sale and offering, exposing or advertising for sale;

    (b) consigning, delivering or serving by way of sale;

    (c) preparing for sale or presenting, labelling or wrapping for the purpose of sale;

    (d) storing or transporting for the purpose of sale;

    (e) importing and exporting;

and, in relation to any food source, means deriving food from it for the purpose of sale or for purposes connected with sale;

"contact material" means any article or substance which is intended to come into contact with food;

"food business" means any business in the course of which commercial operations with respect to food or food sources are carried out;

"food premises" means any premises used for the purposes of a food business;

"food source" means any growing crop or live animal, bird or fish from which food is intended to be derived (whether by harvesting, slaughtering, milking, collecting eggs or otherwise);

"premises" includes any place, any vehicle, stall or moveable structure and, for such purposes as may be specified in an order made by the Ministers, any ship or aircraft of a description so specified.

(4) The reference in subsection (3) above to preparing for sale shall be construed, in relation to any contact material, as a reference to manufacturing or producing for the purpose of sale.

2.—(1) For the purposes of this Act—

6–03

 (a) the supply of food, otherwise than on sale, in the course of a business; and

 (b) any other thing which is done with respect to food and is specified in an order made by the Ministers,

shall be deemed to be a sale of the food, and references to purchasers and purchasing shall be construed accordingly.

(2) This Act shall apply—

 (a) in relation to any food which is offered as a prize or reward or given away in connection with any entertainment to which the public are admitted, whether on payment of money or not, as if the food were, or had been, exposed for sale by each person concerned in the organisation of the entertainment;

 (b) in relation to any food which, for the purpose of advertisement or in furtherance of any trade or business, is offered as a prize or reward or given away, as if the food were, or had been, exposed for sale by the person offering or giving away the food; and

 (c) in relation to any food which is exposed or deposited in any premises for the purpose of being so offered or given away as mentioned in paragraph (a) or (b) above, as if the food were, or had been, exposed for sale by the occupier of the premises;

and in this subsection "entertainment" includes any social gathering, amusement, exhibition, performance, game, sport or trial of skill.

3.—(1) The following provisions shall apply for the purposes of this Act.

6–04

(2) Any food commonly used for human consumption shall, if sold or offered, exposed or kept for sale, be presumed, until the contrary is proved, to have been sold or, as the case may be, to have been or to be intended for sale for human consumption.

(3) The following, namely—

 (a) any food commonly used for human consumption which is found on premises used for the preparation, storage, or sale of that food; and

 (b) any article or substance commonly used in the manufacture of food for human consumption which is found on premises used for the preparation, storage or sale of that food,

shall be presumed, until the contrary is proved, to be intended for sale, or for manufacturing food for sale, for human consumption.

(4) Any article or substance capable of being used in the composition or preparation of any food commonly used for human consumption which is found on premises on which that food is prepared shall, until the contrary is proved, be presumed to be intended for such use.

4.—(1) In this Act—

6–05

'the Minister" means, subject to subsection (2) below—

111

    (a) in relation to England and Wales, the Minister of Agriculture, Fisheries and Food or the Secretary of State;

    (b) in relation to Scotland, the Secretary of State;

'the Ministers" means—

    (a) in relation to England and Wales, the following Ministers acting jointly, namely, the Minister of Agriculture, Fisheries and Food and the Secretaries of State respectively concerned with health in England and food and health in Wales;

    (b) in relation to Scotland, the Secretary of State.

(2) In this Act, in its application to emergency control orders, "the Minister" means the Minister of Agriculture, Fisheries and Food or the Secretary of State.

6–06   5.—(1) Subject to subsections (3) and (4) below, the food authorities in England and Wales are—

    (a) as respects each London borough, district or non-metropolitan county, the council of that borough, district or county;

    (b) as respects the City of London (including the Temples), the Common Council;

    (c) as respects the Inner Temple or the Middle Temple, the appropriate Treasurer.

(2) Subject to subsection 3(a) below, the food authorities in Scotland are the islands or district councils.

(3) Where any functions under this Act are assigned—

    (a) by an order under section 2 or 7 of the Public Health (Control of Disease) Act 1984, to a port health authority or, by an order under section 172 of the Public Health (Scotland) Act 1897, to a port local authority;

    (b) by an order under section 6 of the Public Health Act 1936, to a joint board for a united district; or

    (c) by an order under paragraph 15(6) of Schedule 8 to the Local Government Act 1985, to a single authority for a metropolitan county,

any reference in this Act to a food authority shall be construed, so far as relating to those functions, as a reference to the authority to whom they are so assigned.

(4) The Ministers may by order provide, either generally or in relation to cases of a particular description, that any functions under this Act which are exercisable concurrently—

    (a) as respects a non-metropolitan district, by the council of that district and the council of the non-metropolitan county;

    (b) as respects the Inner Temple or the Middle Temple, by the appropriate Treasurer and the Common Council,

shall be exercisable solely by such one of those authorities as may be specified in the order.

(5) In this section—

'the appropriate Treasurer" means the Sub-Treasurer in relation to the Inner Temple and the Under Treasurer in relation to the Middle Temple;

'the Common Council" means the Common Council of the City of London;

'port local authority" includes a joint port local authority.

(6) In this Act "authorised officer", in relation to a food authority, means any person (whether or not an officer of the authority) who is authorised by them in writing, either generally or specially, to act in matters arising under this Act; but if regulations made by the Ministers so provide, no person shall be so authorised unless he has such qualifications as may be prescribed by the regulations.

6.—(1) In this Act "the enforcement authority", in relation to any provisions of this Act or any regulations or orders made under it, means the authority by whom they are to be enforced and executed.   **6–07**

(2) Every food authority shall enforce and execute within their area the provisions of this Act with respect to which the duty is not imposed expressly or by necessary implication on some other authority.

(3) The Ministers may direct, in relation to cases of a particular description or a particular case, that any duty imposed on food authorities by subsection (2) above shall be discharged by the Ministers or the Minister and not by those authorities.

(4) Regulations or orders under this Act shall specify which of the following authorities are to enforce and execute them, either generally or in relation to cases of a particular description or a particular area, namely—

    (a) the Ministers, the Minister, food authorities and such other authorities as are mentioned in section 5(3) above; and

    (b) in the case of regulations, the Commissioners of Customs and Excise;

and any such regulations or orders may provide for the giving of assistance and information, by any authority concerned in the administration of the regulations or orders, or of any provisions of this Act, to any other authority so concerned, for the purposes of their respective duties under them.

(5) An enforcement authority in England and Wales may institute proceedings under any provisions of this Act or any regulations or orders made under it and, in the case of the Ministers or the Minister, may take over the conduct of any such proceedings which have been instituted by some other person.

PART II

MAIN PROVISIONS

Food safety

7.—(1) Any person who renders any food injurious to health by means of any of the following operations, namely—   **6–08**

    (a) adding any article or substance to the food;

(b) using any article or substance as an ingredient in the preparation of the food;

(c) abstracting any constituent from the food; and

(d) subjecting the food to any other process or treatment.

with intent that it shall be sold for human consumption, shall be guilty of an offence.

(2) In determining for the purposes of this section and section 8(2) below whether any food in injurious to health, regard shall be had—

(a) not only to the probable effect of food on the health of a person consuming it; but

(b) also to the probable cumulative effect of food of substantially the same composition on the health of a person consuming it in ordinary quantities.

(3) In this Part "injury", in relation to health, includes any impairment, whether permanent or temporary, and "injurious to health" shall be construed accordingly.

6–09   8.—Any person who—

(a) sells for human consumption, or offers, exposes or advertises for sale for such consumption, or has in his possession for the purpose of such sale or of preparation for such sale; or

(b) deposits with, or consigns to, any other person for the purpose of such sale or of preparation for such sale,

any food which fails to comply with food safety requirements shall be guilty of an offence.

(2) For the purposes of this Part food fails to comply with food safety requirements if—

(a) it has been rendered injurious to health by means of any of the operations mentioned in section 7(1) above;

(b) it is unfit for human consumption; or

(c) it is so contaminated (whether by extraneous matter or otherwise) that it would not be reasonable to expect it to be used for human consumption in that state;

and references to such requirements or to food complying with such requirements shall be construed accordingly.

(3) Where any food which fails to comply with food safety requirements is part of a batch, lot or consignment of food of the same class or description, it shall be presumed for the purposes of this section and section 9 below, until the contrary is proved, that all of the food in that batch, lot or consignment fails to comply with those requirements.

(4) For the purposes of this Part, any part of, or product derived wholly or partly from, an animal—

(a) which has been slaughtered in a knacker's yard, or of which the carcase has been brought into a knacker's yard; or

(b) in Scotland, which has been slaughtered otherwise than in a slaughterhouse,

shall be deemed to be unfit for human consumption.

(5) In subsection (4) above, in its application to Scotland, "animal" means any description of cattle, sheep, goat, swine, horse, ass or mule; and paragraph (b) of that subsection shall not apply where accident, illness or emergency affecting the animal in question required it to be slaughtered as mentioned in that paragraph.

9.—(1) An authorised officer of a food authority may at all reasonable times **6–10** inspect any food intended for human consumption which—

(a) has been sold or is offered or exposed for sale; or
(b) is in the possession of, or has been deposited with or consigned to, any person for the purpose of sale or of preparation for sale;

and subsections (3) to (9) below shall apply where, on such an inspection, it appears to the authorised officer that any food fails to comply with food safety requirements.

(2) The following provisions shall also apply where, otherwise than on such an inspection, it appears to an authorised officer of a food authority that any food is likely to cause food poisoning or any disease communicable to human beings.

(3) The authorised officer may either—

(a) give notice to the person in charge of the food that, until the notice is withdrawn, the food or any specified portion of it—
   (i) is not to be used for human consumption; and
   (ii) either is not to be removed or is not to be removed except to some place specified in the notice; or
(b) seize the food and remove it in order to have it dealt with by a justice of the peace;

and any person who knowingly contravenes the requirements of a notice under paragraph (a) above shall be guilty of an offence.

(4) Where the authorised officer exercises the powers conferred by subsection (3)(a) above, he shall, as soon as is reasonably practicable and in any event within 21 days, determine whether or not he is satisfied that the food complies with food safety requirements and—

(a) if he is so satisfied, shall forthwith withdraw the notice;
(b) if he is not so satisfied, shall seize the food and remove it in order to have it dealt with by a justice of the peace.

(5) Where an authorised officer exercises the powers conferred by subsection (3)(b) or (4)(b) above, he shall inform the person in charge of the food of his intention to have it dealt with by a justice of the peace and—

(a) any person who under section 7 or 8 above might be liable to a prosecution in respect of the food shall, if he attends before the justice of the peace by whom the food falls to be dealt with, be entitled to be heard and to call witnesses; and

(b) that justice of the peace may, but need not, be a member of the court before which any person is charged with an offence under that section in relation to that food.

(6) If it appears to a justice of the peace, on the basis of such evidence as he considers appropriate in the circumstances, that any food falling to be dealt with by him under this section fails to comply with food safety requirements, he shall condemn the food and order—

(a) the food to be destroyed or to be so disposed of as to prevent it from being used for human consumption; and
(b) any expenses reasonably incurred in connection with the destruction or disposal to be defrayed by the owner of the food.

(7) If a notice under subsection (3)(a) above is withdrawn, or the justice of the peace by whom any food falls to be dealt with under this section refuses to condemn it, the food authority shall compensate the owner of the food for any depreciation in its value resulting from the action taken by the authorised officer.

(8) Any disputed question as to the right to or the amount of any compensation payable under subsection (7) above shall be determined by arbitration.

(9) In the application of this section to Scotland—

(a) any reference to a justice of the peace includes a reference to the sheriff and to a magistrate;
(b) paragraph (b) of subsection (5) above shall not apply;
(c) any order made under subsection (6) above shall be sufficient evidence in any proceedings under this Act of the failure of the food in question to comply with food safety requirements; and
(d) the reference in subsection (8) above to determination by arbitration shall be construed as a reference to determination by a single arbiter appointed, failing agreement between the parties, by the sheriff.

6–11   **10.**—(1) If an authorised officer of an enforcement authority has reasonable grounds for believing that the proprietor of a food business is failing to comply with any regulations to which this section applies, he may, by a notice served on that proprietor (in this Act referred to as an "improvement notice")—

(a) state the officer's grounds for believing that the proprietor is failing to comply with the regulations;
(b) specify the matters which constitute the proprietor's failure so to comply;
(c) specify the measures which, in the officer's opinion, the proprietor must take in order to secure compliance; and
(d) require the proprietor to take those measures, or measures which are at least equivalent to them, within such period (not being less than 14 days) as may be specified in the notice.

(2) Any person who fails to comply with an improvement notice shall be guilty of an offence.

(3) This section and section 11 below apply to any regulations under this Part which make provision—

116

(a) for requiring, prohibiting or regulating the use of any process or treatment in the preparation of food; or

(b) for securing the observance of hygienic conditions and practices in connection with the carrying out of commercial operations with respect to food or food sources.

11.—(1) If—   6–12

(a) the proprietor of a food business is convicted of an offence under any regulations to which this section applies; and

(b) the court by or before which he is so convicted is satisfied that the health risk condition is fulfilled with respect to that business,

the court shall by an order impose the appropriate prohibition.

(2) The health risk condition is fulfilled with respect to any food business if any of the following involves risk of injury to health, namely—

(a) the use for the purposes of the business of any process or treatment;

(b) the construction of any premises used for the purposes of the business, or the use for those purposes of any equipment; and

(c) the state or condition of any premises or equipment used for the purposes of the business.

(3) The appropriate prohibition is—

(a) in a case falling within paragraph (a) of subsection (2) above, a prohibition on the use of the process or treatment for the purposes of the business;

(b) in a case falling within paragraph (b) of that subsection, a prohibition on the use of the premises or equipment for the purposes of the business or any other food business of the same class or description;

(c) in a case falling within paragraph (c) of that subsection, a prohibition on the use of the premises or equipment for the purposes of any food business.

(4) If—

(a) the proprietor of a food business is convicted of an offence under any regulations to which this section applies by virtue of section 10(3)(b) above; *and*

(b) the court by or before which he is so convicted thinks it proper to do so in all the circumstances of the case,

the court may, by an order, impose a prohibition on the proprietor participating in the management of any food business, or any food business of a calls or description specified in the order.

(5) As soon as practicable after the making of an order under subsection (1) or (4) above (in this Act referred to as a "prohibition order"), the enforcement authority shall—

(a) serve a copy of the order on the proprietor of the business; and

(b) in the case of an order under subsection (1) above, affix a copy of the order in a conspicuous position on such premises used for the purposes of the business as they consider appropriate;

117

and any person who knowingly contravenes such an order shall be guilty of an offence.

(6) A prohibition order shall cease to have effect—

    (a) in the case of an order under subsection (1) above, on the issue by the enforcement authority of a certificate to the effect that they are satisfied that the proprietor has taken sufficient measures to secure that the health risk condition is no longer fulfilled with respect to the business;

    (b) in the case of an order under subsection (4) above, on the giving by the court of a direction to that effect.

(7) The enforcement authority shall issue a certificate under paragraph (a) of subsection (6) above within three days of their being satisfied as mentioned in that paragraph; and on an application by the proprietor for such a certificate, the authority shall—

    (a) determine, as soon as is reasonably practicable and in any event within 14 days, whether or not they are so satisfied; and

    (b) if they determine that they are not so satisfied, give notice to the proprietor of the reasons for that determination.

(8) The court shall give a direction under subsection (6)(b) above if, on an application by the proprietor, the court thinks it proper to do so having regard to all the circumstances of the case, including in particular the conduct of the proprietor since the making of the order; but no such application shall be entertained if it is made—

    (a) within six months after the making of the prohibition order; or

    (b) within three months after the making by the proprietor of a previous application for such a direction.

(9) Where a magistrates' court or, in Scotland, the sheriff makes an order under section 12(2) below with respect to any food business, subsection (1) above shall apply as if the proprietor of the business had been convicted by the court or sheriff of an offence under regulations to which this section applies.

(10) Subsection (4) above shall apply in relation to a manager of a food business as it applies in relation to the proprietor of such a business; and any reference in subsection (5) or (8) above to the proprietor of the business, or to the proprietor, shall be construed accordingly.

(11) In subsection (10) above "manager", in relation to a food business, means any person who is entrusted by the proprietor with the day to day running of the business, or any part of the business.

6–13   **12.**—(1) If an authorised officer of an enforcement authority is satisfied that the health risk condition is fulfilled with respect to any food business, he may, by a notice served on the proprietor of the business (in this Act referred to as an "emergency prohibition notice"), impose the appropriate prohibition.

(2) If a magistrates' court or, in Scotland, the sheriff is satisfied, on the application of such an officer, that the health risk condition is fulfilled with respect to any food business, the court or sheriff shall, by an order (in this Act referred to as an "emergency prohibition order"), impose the appropriate prohibition.

(3) Such an officer shall not apply for an emergency prohibition order unless, at least one day before the date of the application, he has served notice on the proprietor of the business of his intention to apply for the order.

(4) Subsections (2) and (3) of section 11 above shall apply for the purposes of this section as they apply for the purposes of that section, but as if the reference in subsection (2) to risk of injury to health were a reference to imminent risk of such injury.

(5) As soon as practicable after the service of an emergency prohibition notice, the enforcement authority shall affix a copy of the notice in a conspicuous position on such premises used for the purposes of the business as they consider appropriate; and any person who knowingly contravenes such a notice shall be guilty of an offence.

(6) As soon as practicable after the making of an emergency prohibition order, the enforcement authority shall—

(a) serve a copy of the order on the proprietor of the business; and
(b) affix a copy of the order in a conspicuous position on such premises used for the purposes of that business as they consider appropriate;

and any person who knowingly contravenes such an order shall be guilty of an offence.

(7) An emergency prohibition notice shall cease to have effect—

(a) if no application for an emergency prohibition order is made within the period of three days beginning with the service of the notice, at the end of that period;
(b) if such an application is so made, on the determination or abandonment of the application.

(8) An emergency prohibition notice or emergency prohibition order shall cease to have effect on the issue by the enforcement authority of a certificate to the effect that they are satisfied that the proprietor has taken sufficient measures to secure that the health risk condition is no longer fulfilled with respect to the business.

(9) The enforcement authority shall issue a certificate under subsection (8) above within three days of their being satisfied as mentioned in that subsection; and on an application by the proprietor for such a certificate, the authority shall—

(a) determine, as soon as is reasonably practicable and in any event within 14 days, whether or not they are so satisfied; and
(b) if they determine that they are not so satisfied, give notice to the proprietor of the reasons for that determination.

119

(10) Where an emergency prohibition notice is served on the proprietor of a business, the enforcement authority shall compensate him in respect of any loss suffered by reason of his complying with the notice unless—

(a) an application for an emergency prohibition order is made within the period of three days beginning with the service of the notice; and
(b) the court declares itself satisfied, on the hearing of the application, that the health risk condition was fulfilled with respect to the business at the time when the notice was served;

and any disputed question as to the right to or the amount of any compensation payable under this subsection shall be determined by arbitration or, in Scotland, by a single arbiter appointed, failing agreement between the parties, by the sheriff.

6–14   **13.**—(1) If it appears to the Minister that the carrying out of commercial operations with respect to food, food sources or contact materials of any class or description involves or may involve imminent risk of injury to health, he may, by an order (in this Act referred to as an "emergency control order"), prohibit the carrying out of such operations with respect to food, food sources or contact materials of that class or description.

(2) Any person who knowingly contravenes an emergency control order shall be guilty of an offence.

(3) The Minister may consent, either unconditionally or subject to any condition that he considers appropriate, to the doing in a particular case of anything prohibited by an emergency control order.

(4) It shall be a defence for a person charged with an offence under subsection (2) above to show—

(a) that consent had been given under subsection (3) above to the contravention of the emergency control order; and
(b) that any condition subject to which that consent was given was complied with.

(5) The Minister—

(a) may give such directions as appear to him to be necessary or expedient for the purpose of preventing the carrying out of commercial operations with respect to any food, food sources or contact materials which he believes, on reasonable grounds, to be food, food sources or contact materials to which an emergency control order applies; and
(b) may do anything which appears to him to be necessary or expedient for that purpose.

(6) Any person who fails to comply with a direction under this section shall be guilty of an offence.

(7) If the Minister does anything by virtue of this section in consequence of any person failing to comply with an emergency control order or a direction under this section, the Minister may recover from that person any expenses reasonably incurred by him under this section.

Consumer protection

14.—(1) Any person who sells to the purchaser's prejudice any food which is not   **6–15**
of the nature or substance or quality demanded by the purchaser shall be guilty of an
offence.

(2) In subsection (1) above the reference to sale shall be construed as a reference
to sale for human consumption; and in proceedings under that subsection it shall
not be a defence that the purchaser was not prejudiced because he bought for
analysis or examination.

15.—(1) Any person who gives with any food sold by him, or displays with any   **6–16**
food offered or exposed by him for sale or in his possession for the purpose of sale, a
label, whether or not attached to or printed on the wrapper or container, which—

    (a) falsely describes the food; or
    (b) is likely to mislead as to the nature or substance or quality of the food;

shall be guilty of an offence.

(2) Any person who publishes, or is a party to the publication of, an advertisement (not being such a label given or displayed by him as mentioned in subsection
(1) above) which—

    (a) falsely describes any food; or
    (b) is likely to mislead as to the nature or substance or quality of any food,

shall be guilty of an offence.

(3) Any person who sells, or offers or exposes for sale, or has in his possession for
the purpose of sale, any food the presentation of which is likely to mislead as to the
nature or substance or quality of the food shall be guilty of an offence.

(4) In proceedings for an offence under subsection (1) or (2) above, the fact that a
label or advertisement in respect of which the offence is alleged to have been
committed contained an accurate statement of the composition of the food shall not
preclude the court from finding that the offence was committed.

(5) In this section references to sale shall be construed as references to sale for
human consumption.

Regulations

16.—(1) The Ministers may by regulations make—   **6–17**

    (a) provision for requiring, prohibiting or regulating the presence in food or
        food sources of any specified substance, or any substance of any specified
        class, and generally for regulating the composition of food;
    (b) provision for securing that food is fit for human consumption and meets
        such microbiological standards (whether going to the fitness of the food or
        otherwise) as may be specified by or under the regulations;

(c) provision for requiring, prohibiting or regulating the use of any process or treatment in the preparation of food;

(d) provision for securing the observance of hygienic conditions and practices in connection with the carrying out of commercial operations with respect to food or food sources;

(e) provision for imposing requirements or prohibitions as to, or otherwise regulating, the labelling, marking, presenting or advertising of food, and the descriptions which may be applied to food; and

(f) such other provision with respect to food or food sources, including in particular provision for prohibiting or regulating the carrying out of commercial operations with respect to food or food sources, as appears to them to be necessary or expedient—

    (i) for the purpose of securing that food complies with food safety requirements or in the interests of the public health; or

    (ii) for the purpose of protecting or promoting the interests of consumers.

(2) The Ministers may also by regulations make provision—

(a) for securing the observance of hygienic conditions and practices in connection with the carrying out of commercial operations with respect to contact materials which are intended to come into contact with food intended for human consumption;

(b) for imposing requirements or prohibitions as to, or otherwise regulating, the labelling, marking or advertising of such materials, and the descriptions which may be applied to them; and

(c) otherwise for prohibiting or regulating the carrying out of commercial operations with respect to such materials.

(3) Without prejudice to the generality of subsection (1) above, regulations under that subsection may make any such provision as is mentioned in Schedule 1 to this Act.

(4) In making regulations under subsection (1) above, the Ministers shall have regard to the desirability of restricting, so far as practicable, the use of substances of no nutritional value as foods or as ingredients of foods.

(5) In subsection (1) above and Schedule 1 to this Act, unless the context otherwise requires—

(a) references to food shall be construed as references to food intended for sale for human consumption; and

(b) references to food sources shall be construed as references to food sources from which such food is intended to be derived.

6–18   17.—(1) The Ministers may by regulations make such provision with respect to food, food sources or contact materials, including in particular provision for prohibiting or regulating the carrying out of commercial operations with respect to food, food sources or contact materials, as appears to them to be called for by any Community obligation.

(2) As respects any directly applicable Community provision which relates to food, food sources or contact materials and for which, in their opinion, it is appropriate to provide under this Act, the Ministers may by regulations—

(a) make such provision as they consider necessary or expedient for the purpose of securing that the Community provision is administered, executed and enforced under this Act; and

(b) apply such of the provisions of this Act as may be specified in the regulations in relation to the Community provision with such modifications, if any, as may be so specified.

(3) In subsections (1) and (2) above references to food or food sources shall be construed in accordance with section 16(5) above.

18.—The Ministers may by regulations make provision—   **6–19**

(a) for prohibiting the carrying out of commercial operations with respect to novel foods, or food sources from which such foods are intended to be derived, of any class specified in the regulations;

(b) for prohibiting the carrying out of such operations with respect to genetically modified food sources, or foods derived from such food sources, of any class so specified; or

(c) for prohibiting the importation of any food of a class so specified,

and (in each case) for excluding from the prohibition any food or food source which is of a description specified by or under the regulations and, in the case of a prohibition on importation, is imported at an authorised place of entry.

(2) The Ministers may also by regulations—

(a) prescribe, in relation to milk of any description, such a designation (in this subsection referred to as a "special designation") as the Ministers consider appropriate;

(b) provide for the issue by enforcement authorities of licences to producers and sellers of milk authorising the use of a special designation; and

(c) prohibit, without the use of a special designation, all sales of milk for human consumption, other than sales made with the Minister's consent.

(3) In this section—

"authorised place of entry" means any port, aerodrome or other place of entry authorised by or under the regulations and, in relation to food in a particular consignment, includes any place of entry so authorised for the importation of that consignment;

"description", in relation to food, includes any description of its origin or of the manner in which it is packed;

"novel food" means any food which has not previously been used for human consumption in Great Britain, or has been so used only to a very limited extent.

(4) For the purposes of this section a food source is genetically modified if any of the genes or other genetic material in the food source—

(a) has been modified by means of an artificial technique; or

(b) is inherited or otherwise derived, through any number of replications, from genetic material which was so modified;

123

and in this subsection "artificial technique" does not include any technique which involves no more than, or no more than the assistance of, naturally occurring processes of reproduction (including selective breeding techniques or *in vitro* fertilisation).

6–20 **19.**—(1) The Ministers may by regulations make provision—

(a) for the registration by enforcement authorities of premises used or proposed to be used for the purposes of a food business, and for prohibiting the use for those purposes of any premises which are not registered in accordance with the regulations; or

(b) subject to subsection (2) below, for the issue by such authorities of licences in respect of the use of premises for the purposes of a food business, and for prohibiting the use for those purposes of any premises except in accordance with a licence issued under the regulations.

(2) The Ministers shall exercise the power conferred by subsection (1)(b) above only where it appears to them to be necessary or expedient to do so—

(a) for the purpose of securing that food complies with food safety requirements or in the interests of the public health; or

(b) for the purpose of protecting or promoting the interests of consumers.

Defences etc.

6–21 **20.** Where the commission by any person of an offence under any of the preceding provisions of this Part is due to an act or default of some other person, that other person shall be guilty of the offence; and a person may be charged with and convicted of the offence by virtue of this section whether or not proceedings are taken against the first-mentioned person.

6–22 **21.**—(1) In any proceedings for an offence under any of the preceding provisions of this Part (in this section referred to as "the relevant provision"), it shall, subject to subsection (5) below, be a defence for the person charged to prove that he took all reasonable precautions and exercised all due diligence to avoid the commission of the offence by himself or by a person under his control.

(2) Without prejudice to the generality of subsection (1) above, a person charged with an offence under section 8, 14 or 15 above who neither—

(a) prepared the food in respect of which the offence is alleged to have been committed; nor

(b) imported it into Great Britain,

shall be taken to have established the defence provided by that subsection if he satisfied the requirements of subsection (3) or (4) below.

(3) A person satisfied the requirements of this subsection if he proves—

(a) that the commission of the offence was due to an act or default of another person who was not under his control, or to reliance on information supplied by such a person;

(b) that he carried out all such checks of the food in question as were reasonable in all the circumstances, or that it was reasonable in all the circumstances for him to rely on checks carried out by the person who supplied the food to him; and

(c) that he did not know and had no reason to suspect at the time of the commission of the alleged offence that his act or omission would amount to an offence under the relevant provision.

(4) A person satisfies the requirements of this subsection if he proves—

(a) that the commission of the offence was due to an act or default of another person who was not under his control, or to reliance on information supplied by such a person;

(b) that the sale or intended sale of which the alleged offence consisted was not a sale or intended sale under his name or mark; and

(c) that he did not know, and could not reasonably have been expected to know, at the time of the commission of the alleged offence that his act or omission would amount to an offence under the relevant provision.

(5) If in any case the defence provided by subsection (1) above involves the allegation that the commission of the offence was due to an act or default of another person, or to reliance on information supplied by another person, the person charged shall not, without leave of the court, be entitled to rely on that defence unless—

(a) at least seven clear days before the hearing; and

(b) where he has previously appeared before a court in connection with the alleged offence, within one month of his first such appearance,

he has served on the prosecutor a notice in writing giving such information identifying or assisting in the identification of that other person as was then in his possession.

(6) In subsection (5) above any reference to appearing before a court shall be construed as including a reference to being brought before a court.

22.—In proceedings for an offence under any of the preceding provisions of this Part consisting of the advertisement for sale of any food, it shall be a defence for the person charged to prove— **6–23**

(a) that he is a person whose business it is to publish or arrange for the publication of advertisements; and

(b) that he received the advertisement in the ordinary course of business and did not know and had no reason to suspect that its publication would amount to an offence under that provision.

Miscellaneous and supplemental

23.—(1) A food authority may provide, whether within or outside their area, training courses in food hygiene for persons who are or intend to become involved in food businesses, whether as proprietors or employees or otherwise. **6–24**

(2) A food authority may contribute towards the expenses incurred under this section by any other such authority, or towards expenses incurred by any other person in providing, such courses as are mentioned in subsection (1) above.

6–25 **24.**—(1) A food authority may provide, whether within or outside their area, tanks or other apparatus for cleansing shellfish.

(2) A food authority may contribute towards the expenses incurred under this section by any other such authority, or towards expenses incurred by any other person in providing, and making available to the public, tanks or other apparatus for cleansing shellfish.

(3) Nothing in this section authorises the establishment of any tank or other apparatus, or the execution of any other work, on, over or under tidal lands below high-water mark or ordinary spring tides, except in accordance with such plans and sections, and subject to such restrictions and conditions as may before the work is commenced be approved by the Secretary of State.

(4) In this section "cleansing", in relation to shellfish, includes subjecting them to any germicidal treatment.

6–26 **25.**—(1) For the purpose of facilitating the exercise of their functions under this Part, the Ministers may by order require every person who at the date of the order, or at any subsequent time, carries on a business of a specified class or description (in this section referred to as a "relevant business")—

- (a) to afford to persons specified in the order such facilities for the taking of samples of any food, substance or contact material to which subsection (2) below applies; or
- (b) to furnish to persons so specified such information concerning any such food, substance or contact material,

as (in each case) is specified in the order and is reasonably required by such persons.

(2) This subsection applies to—

- (a) any food of a class specified in the order which is sold or intended to be sold in the course of a relevant business for human consumption;
- (b) any substance of a class so specified which is sold in the course of such a business for use in the preparation of food for human consumption, or is used for that purpose in the course of such a business; and
- (c) any contact material of a class so specified which is sold in the course of such a business and is intended to come into contact with food intended for human consumption.

(3) No information relating to any individual business which is obtained by means of an order under subsection (1) above shall, without the previous consent in writing of the person carrying on the business, be disclosed except—

- (a) in accordance with directions of the Minister, so far as may be necessary for the purposes of this Act or of any corresponding enactment in force in Northern Ireland, or for the purpose of complying with any Community obligation; or

(b) for the purposes of any proceedings for an offence against the order or any report of those proceedings;

and any person who discloses any such information in contravention of this subsection shall be guilty of an offence.

(4) In subsection (3) above the reference to a disclosure being necessary for the purposes of this Act includes a reference to it being necessary—

(a) for the purpose of securing that food complies with food safety requirements or in the interests of the public health; or
(b) for the purpose of protecting or promoting the interests of consumers;

and the reference to a disclosure being necessary for the purposes of any corresponding enactment in force in Northern Ireland shall be construed accordingly.

26.—(1) Regulations under this Part may— **6–27**

(a) make provision for prohibiting or regulating the carrying out of commercial operations with respect to any food, food source or contact material—
  (i) which fails to comply with the regulations; or
  (ii) in relation to which an offence against the regulations has been committed, or would have been committed if any relevant act or omission had taken place in Great Britain; and
(b) without prejudice to the generality of section 9 above, provide that any food which, in accordance with the regulations, is certified as being such food as is mentioned in paragraph (a) above may be treated for the purposes of that section as failing to comply with food safety requirements.

(2) Regulations under this Part may also—

(a) require persons carrying on any activity to which the regulations apply to keep and produce records and provide returns;
(b) prescribe the particulars to be entered on any register required to be kept in accordance with the regulations;
(c) require any such register to be open to inspection by the public at all reasonable times and, subject to that, authorise it to be kept by means of a computer;
(d) prescribe the periods for which and the conditions subject to which licences may be issued, and provide for the subsequent alteration of conditions and for the cancellation, suspension or revocation of licences;
(e) provide for an appeal to a magistrates' court or, in Scotland, to the sheriff, or to a tribunal constituted in accordance with the regulations, against any decision of an enforcement authority, or of an authorised officer of such an authority; and
(f) provide, as respects any appeal to such a tribunal, for the procedure on the appeal (including costs) and for any appeal against the tribunal's decision.

(3) Regulations under this Part or an order under section 25 above may—

(a) provide that an offence under the regulations or order shall be triable in such way as may be there specified; and

127

(b) include provisions under which a person guilty of such an offence shall be liable to such penalties (not exceeding those which may be imposed in respect of offences under this Act) as may be specified in the regulations or order.

PART III

ADMINISTRATION AND ENFORCEMENT

Administration

6–28 **27.**—(1) Every authority to whom this section applies, that is to say, every food authority in England and Wales and every regional or islands council in Scotland, shall appoint in accordance with this section one or more persons (in this Act referred to as "public analysts") to act as analysts for the purposes of this Act within the authority's area.

(2) No person shall be appointed as a public analyst unless he possesses—

(a) such qualifications as may be prescribed by regulations made by the Ministers; or
(b) such other qualifications as the Ministers may approve,

and no person shall act as a public analyst for any area who is engaged directly or indirectly in any food business which is carried on in that area.

(3) An authority to whom this section applies shall pay to a public analyst such remuneration as may be agreed, which may be expressed to be payable either—

(a) in addition to any fees received by him under this Part; or
(b) on condition that any fees so received by him are paid over by him to the authority.

(4) An authority to whom this section applies who appoint only one public analyst may appoint also a deputy to act during any vacancy in the office of public analyst, or during the absence or incapacity of the holder of the office, and—

(a) the provisions of this section with respect to the qualifications, appointment, removal and remuneration of a public analyst shall apply also in relation to a deputy public analyst; and
(b) any reference in the following provisions of this Act to a public analyst shall be construed as including a reference to a deputy public analyst appointed under this subsection.

(5) In subsection (1) above "food authority" does not include the council of a non-metropolitan district, the Sub-Treasurer of the Inner Temple or the Under Treasurer of the Middle Temple; and in subsection (2) above the reference to being engaged directly or indirectly in a food business includes a reference to having made such arrangements with a food business as may be prescribed by regulations made by the Ministers.

28.—(1) A food authority, or a regional council in Scotland, may provide facilities   **6–29**
for examinations for the purposes of this Act.

(2) In this Act "examination" means a microbiological examination and "examine" shall be construed accordingly.

Sampling and analysis etc.

29. An authorised officer of an enforcement authority may—   **6–30**

(a) purchase a sample of any food, or any substance capable of being used in the preparation of food;
(b) take a sample of any food, or any such substance, which—
  (i) appears to him to be intended for sale, or to have been sold, for human consumption; or
  (ii) is found by him on or in any premises which he is authorised to enter by or under section 32 below;
(c) take a sample from any food source, or a sample of any contact material, which is found by him on or in any such premises;
(d) take a sample of any article or substance which is found by him on or in any such premises and which he has reason to believe may be required as evidence in proceedings under any of the provisions of this Act or of regulations or orders made under it.

30.—(1) An authorised officer of an enforcement authority who has procured a   **6–31**
sample under section 29 above shall—

(a) if he considers that the sample should be analysed, submit it to be analysed either—
  (i) by the public analyst for the area in which the sample was procured; or
  (ii) by the public analyst for the area which consists of or includes the area of the authority;
(b) if he considers that the sample should be examined, submit it to be examined by a food examiner.

(2) A person, other than such an officer, who has purchased any food, or any substance capable of being used in the preparation of food, may submit a sample of it—

(a) to be analysed by the public analyst for the area in which the purchase was made; or
(b) to be examined by a food examiner.

(3) If, in any case where a sample is proposed to be submitted for analysis under this section, the office of public analyst for the area in question is vacant, the sample shall be submitted to the public analyst for some other area.

(4) If, in any case where a sample is proposed to be or is submitted for analysis or examination under this section, the food analyst or examiner determines that he is for any reason unable to perform the analysis or examination, the sample shall be submitted or, as the case may be, sent by him to such other food analyst or examiner as he may determine.

(5) A food analyst or examiner shall analyse or examine as soon as practicable any sample submitted or sent to him under this section, but may, except where—

(a) he is the public analyst for the area in question; and
(b) the sample is submitted to him for analysis by an authorised officer of an enforcement authority.

demand in advance the payment of such reasonable fees as he may require.

(6) A food analyst or examiner who has analysed or examined a sample shall give to the person by whom it was submitted a certificate specifying the result of the analysis or examination.

(7) Any certificate given by a food analyst or examiner under subsection (6) above shall be signed by him, but the analysis or examination may be made by any person acting under his direction.

(8) In any proceedings under this Act, the production by one of the parties—

(a) of a document purporting to be a certificate given by a food analyst or examiner under subsection (6) above; or
(b) of a document supplied to him by the other party as being a copy of such a certificate,

shall be sufficient evidence of the facts stated in it unless, in a case falling within paragraph (a) above, the other party requires that the food analyst or examiner shall be called as a witness.

(9) In this section—

'food analyst" means a public analyst or any other person who possesses the requisite qualifications to carry out analyses for the purposes of this Act;

'food examiner" means any person who possesses the requisite qualifications to carry out examinations for the purposes of this Act;

'the requisite qualifications" means such qualifications as may be prescribed by regulations made by the Ministers, or such other qualifications as the Ministers may approve;

'sample", in relation to an authorised officer of an enforcement authority, includes any part of a sample retained by him in pursuance of regulations under section 31 below;

and where two or more public analysts are appointed for any area, any reference in this section to the public analyst for that area shall be construed as a reference to either or any of them.

6–32   **31.**—(1) The Ministers may by regulations make provision for supplementing or modifying the provisions of sections 29 and 30 above.

(2) Without prejudice to the generality of subsection (1) above, regulations under that subsection may make provision with respect to—

(a) the matters to be taken into account in determining whether, and at what times, samples should be procured;

(b) the manner of procuring samples, including the steps to be taken in order to ensure that any samples procured are fair samples;

(c) the method of dealing with samples, including (where appropriate) their division into parts;

(d) the persons to whom parts of samples are to be given and the persons by whom such parts are to be retained;

(e) the notices which are to be given to, and the information which is to be furnished by, the persons in charge of any food, substance, contact material or food source of or from which samples are procured;

(f) the methods which are to be used in analysing or examining samples, or parts of samples, or in classifying the results of analyses or examinations;

(g) the circumstances in which a food analyst or examiner is to be precluded, by reason of a conflict of interest, from analysing or examining a particular sample or part of a sample; and

(h) the circumstances in which samples, or parts of samples, are to be or may be submitted for analysis or examination—

    (i) to the Government Chemist, or to such other food analyst or examiner as he may direct; or

    (ii) to a person determined by or under the regulations.

(3) In this section "food analyst" and "food examiner" have the same meanings as in section 30 above.

Powers of entry and obstruction etc.

32.—(1) An authorised officer of an enforcement authority shall, on producing, if so required, some duly authenticated document showing his authority, have a right at all reasonable hours— **6–33**

(a) to enter any premises within the authority's area for the purpose of ascertaining whether there is or has been on the premises any contravention of the provisions of this Act, or of regulations or orders made under it; and

(b) to enter any business premises, whether within or outside the authority's area, for the purpose of ascertaining whether there is on the premises any evidence of any contravention within that area of any of such provisions; and

(c) in the case of an authorised officer of a food authority, to enter any premises for the purpose of the performance by the authority of their functions under this Act;

but admission to any premises used only as a private dwelling-house shall not be demanded as of right unless 24 hours' notice of the intended entry has been given to the occupier.

(2) If a justice of the peace, on sworn information in writing, is satisfied that there is reasonable ground for entry into any premises for any such purpose as is mentioned in subsection (1) above and either—

(a) that admission to the premises has been refused, or a refusal is appre-hended, and that notice of the intention to apply for a warrant has been given to the occupier; or

(b) that an application for admission, or the giving of such a notice, would defeat the object of the entry, or that the case is one of urgency, or that the premises are unoccupied or the occupier temporarily absent,

the justice may by warrant signed by him authorise the authorised officer to enter the premises, if need be by reasonable force.

(3) Every warrant granted under this section shall continue in force for a period of one month.

(4) An authorised officer entering any premises by virtue of this section, or of a warrant issued under it, may take with him such other persons as he considers necessary, and on leaving any unoccupied premises which he has entered by virtue of such a warrant shall leave them as effectively secured against unauthorised entry as he found them.

(5) An authorised officer entering premises by virtue of this section, or of a warrant issued under it, may inspect any records (in whatever form they are held) relating to a food business and, where any such records are kept by means of a computer—

(a) may have access to, and inspect and check the operation of, any computer and any associated apparatus or material which is or has been in use in connection with the records; and

(b) may require any person having charge of, or otherwise concerned with the operation of, the computer, apparatus or material to afford him such assistance as he may reasonably require.

(6) Any officer exercising any power conferred by subsection (5) above may—

(a) seize and detain any records which he has reason to believe may be required as evidence in proceedings under any of the provisions of this Act or of regulations or orders made under it; and

(b) where the records are kept by means of a computer, may require the records to be produced in a form in which they may be taken away.

(7) If any person who enters any premises by virtue of this section, or of a warrant issued under it, discloses to any person any information obtained by him in the premises with regard to any trade secret, he shall, unless the disclosure was made in the performance of his duty, be guilty of an offence.

(8) Nothing in this section authorises any person, except with the permission of the local authority under the Animal Health Act 1981, to enter any premises—

(a) in which an animal or bird affected with any disease to which that Act applies is kept; and

(b) which is situated in a place declared under that Act to be infected with such a disease.

(9) In the application of this section to Scotland, any reference to a justice of the peace includes a reference to the sheriff and to a magistrate.

33.—(1) Any person who—

6–34

(a) intentionally obstructs any person acting in the execution of this Act; or

(b) without reasonable cause, fails to give to any person acting in the execution of this Act any assistance or information which that person may reasonably require of him for the performance of his functions under this Act,

shall be guilty of an offence.

(2) Any person who, in purported compliance with any such requirement as is mentioned in subsection (1)(b) above—

(a) furnishes information which he knows to be false or misleading in a material particular; or

(b) recklessly furnishes information which is false or misleading in a material particular,

shall be guilty of an offence.

(3) Nothing in subsection (1)(b) above shall be construed as requiring any person to answer any question or give any information if to do so might incriminate him.

Offences

34. No prosecution for an offence under this Act which is punishable under section 35(2) below shall be begun after the expiry of—

6–35

(a) three years from the commission of the offence; or

(b) one year from its discovery by the prosecutor,

whichever is the earlier.

35.—(1) A person guilty of an offence under section 33(1) above shall be liable on summary conviction to a fine not exceeding level 5 on the standard scale or to imprisonment for a term not exceeding three months or to both.

6–36

(2) A person guilty of any other offence under this Act shall be liable—

(a) on conviction on indictment, to a fine or to imprisonment for a term not exceeding two years or to both;

(b) on summary conviction, to a fine not exceeding the relevant amount or to imprisonment for a term not exceeding six months or to both.

(3) In subsection (2) above "the relevant amount" means—

(a) in the case of an offence under section 7, 8 or 14 above, £20,000;

(b) in any other case, the statutory maximum.

(4) If a person who is—

(a) licensed under section 1 of the Slaughterhouses Act 1974 to keep a slaughter house or knacker's yard;

(b) registered under section 4 of the Slaughter of Animals (Scotland) Act 1980 in respect of any premises for use as a slaughterhouse; or

(c) licensed under section 6 of that Act to use any premises as a knacker's yard, is convicted of an offence under Part II of this Act, the court may, in addition to any other punishment, cancel his licence or registration.

6–37   **36.**—(1) Where an offence under this Act which has been committed by a body corporate is proved to have been committed with the consent or connivance of, or to be attributable to any neglect on the part of—

(a) any director, manager, secretary or other similar officer of the body corporate; or
(b) any person who was purporting to act in any such capacity,

he as well as the body corporate shall be deemed to be guilty of that offence and shall be liable to be proceeded against and punished accordingly.

(2) In subsection (1) above "director", in relation to any body corporate established by or under any enactment for the purpose of carrying on under national ownership any industry or part of an industry or undertaking, being a body corporate whose affairs are managed by its members, means a member of that body corporate.

Appeals

6–38   **37.**—(1) Any person who is aggrieved by—

(a) a decision of an authorised officer of an enforcement authority to serve an improvement notice;
(b) a decision of an enforcement authority to refuse to issue such a certificate as is mentioned in section 11(6) or 12(8) above; or
(c) subject to subsection (2) below, a decision of such an authority to refuse, cancel, suspend or revoke a licence required by regulations under Part II of this Act,

may appeal to a magistrates' court or, in Scotland, to the sheriff.

(2) Subsection (1)(c) above shall not apply in relation to any decision as respects which regulations under Part II of this Act provide for an appeal to a tribunal constituted in accordance with the regulations.

(3) The procedure on an appeal to a magistrates' court under subsection (1) above, or an appeal to such a court for which provision is made by regulations under Part II of this Act, shall be by way of complaint for an order, and the Magistrates' Courts Act 1980 shall apply to the proceedings.

(4) An appeal to the sheriff under subsection (1) above, or an appeal to the sheriff for which provision is made by regulations under Part II of this Act, shall be by summary application.

(5) The period within which such an appeal as is mentioned in subsection (3) or (4) above may be brought shall be—

(a) one month from the date on which notice of the decision was served on the person desiring to appeal; or

(b) in the case of an appeal under subsection (1)(a) above, that period or the period specified in the improvement notice, whichever ends the earlier;

and, in the case of such an appeal as is mentioned in subsection (3) above, the making of the complaint shall be deemed for the purposes of this subsection to be the bringing of the appeal.

(6) In any case where such an appeal as is mentioned in subsection (3) or (4) above lies, the document notifying the decision to the person concerned shall state—

(a) the right of appeal to a magistrates' court or to the sheriff; and
(b) the period within which such an appeal may be brought.

38. A person who is aggrieved by—   **6–39**

(a) any dismissal by a magistrates' court of such an appeal as is mentioned in section 37(3) above; or
(b) any decision of such a court to make a prohibition order or an emergency prohibition order, or to exercise the power conferred by section 35(4) above,

may appeal to the Crown Court.

39.—(1) On an appeal against an improvement notice, the court may either cancel   **6–40**
or affirm the notice and, if it affirms it, may do so either in its original form or with such modifications as the court may in the circumstances think fit.

(2) Where, apart from this subsection, any period specified in an improvement notice would include any day on which an appeal against that notice is pending, that day shall be excluded from that period.

(3) An appeal shall be regarded as pending for the purposes of subsection (2) above until it is finally disposed of, is withdrawn or is struck out for want of prosecution.

PART IV

Miscellaneous and Supplemental

Powers of Ministers

40.—(1) For the guidance of food authorities, the Ministers or the Minister may   **6–41**
issue codes of recommended practice as regards the execution and enforcement of this Act and of regulations and orders made under it; and any such code shall be laid before Parliament after being issued.

(2) In the exercise of the functions conferred on them by or under this Act, every food authority—

(a) shall have regard to any relevant provision of any such code; and

(b) shall comply with any direction which is given by the Ministers or the Minister and requires them to take any specified steps in order to comply with such a code.

(3) Any direction under subsection (2)(b) above shall, on the application of the Ministers or the Minister, be enforceable by mandamus or, in Scotland, by an order of the Court of Session under section 45 of the Court of Session Act 1988.

(4) Before issuing any code under this section, the Ministers or the Minister shall consult with such organisations as appear to them or him to be representative of interests likely to be substantially affected by the code.

(5) Any consultation undertaken before the commencement of subsection (4) above shall be as effective, for the purposes of that subsection, as if undertaken after that commencement.

6–42   **41.** Every food authority shall send to the Minister such reports and returns, and give him such information, with respect to the exercise of the functions conferred on them by or under this Act as he may require.

6–43   **42.**—(1) Where the Minister is satisfied that—

(a) a food authority (in this section referred to as "the authority in default") have failed to discharge any duty imposed by or under this Act; and
(b) the authority's failure affects the general interests of consumers of food,

he may by order empower another food authority (in this section referred to as "the substitute authority"), or one of his officers, to discharge that duty in place of the authority in default.

(2) For the purpose of determining whether the power conferred by subsection (1) above is exercisable, the Minister may cause a local inquiry to be held; and where he does so, the relevant provisions of the Local Government Act shall apply as if the inquiry were a local inquiry held under that Act.

(3) Nothing in subsection (1) above affects any other power exercisable by the Minister with respect to defaults of local authorities.

(4) The substitute authority or the Minister may recover from the authority in default any expenses reasonably incurred by them or him under subsection (1) above; and for the purpose of paying any such amount the authority in default may—

(a) raise money as if the expenses had been incurred directly by them as a local authority; and
(b) if and to the extent that they are authorised to do so by the Minister, borrow money in accordance with the statutory provisions relating to borrowing by a local authority.

(5) In this section "the relevant provisions of the Local Government Act" means subsections (2) to (5) of section 250 of the Local Government Act 1972 in relation to England and Wales and subsections (3) to (8) of section 210 of the Local Government (Scotland) Act 1973 in relation to Scotland.

Protective provisions

43.—(1) This section shall have effect on the death of any person who— **6–44**

    (a) is registered in respect of any premises in accordance with regulations made under Part II of this Act; or

    (b) holds a licence issued in accordance with regulations so made.

(2) The registration or licence shall subsist for the benefit of the deceased's personal representative, or his widow or any other member of his family, until the end of—

    (a) the period of three months beginning with his death; or

    (b) such longer period as the enforcement authority may allow.

44.—(1) An officer of a food authority is not personally liable in respect of any act **6–45** done by him—

    (a) in the execution or purported execution of this Act; and

    (b) within the scope of his employment,

if he did that act in the honest belief that his duty under this Act required or entitled him to do it.

(2) Nothing in subsection (1) above shall be construed as relieving any food authority from any liability in respect of the acts of their officers.

(3) Where an action has been brought against an officer of a food authority in respect of an act done by him—

    (a) in the execution or purported execution of this Act; but

    (b) outside the scope of his employment.

the authority may indemnify him against the whole or a part of any damages which he has been ordered to pay or any costs which he may have incurred if they are satisfied that he honestly believed that the act complained of was within the scope of his employment.

(4) A public analyst appointed by a food authority shall be treated for the purposes of this section as being an officer of the authority, whether or not his appointment is a whole-time appointment.

Financial provisions

45.—(1) The Ministers may make regulations requiring or authorising charges to **6–46** be imposed by enforcement authorities in respect of things done by them which they are required or authorised to do by or under this Act.

(2) Regulations under this section may include such provision as the Ministers see fit as regards charges for which the regulations provide and the recovery of such charges; and nothing in the following provisions shall prejudice this.

137

(3) Regulations under this section may provide that the amount of a charge (if imposed) is to be at the enforcement authority's discretion or to be at its discretion subject to a maximum or a minimum.

(4) Regulations under this section providing that a charge may not exceed a maximum amount, or be less than a minimum amount, may—

(a) provide for one amount, or a scale of amounts to cover different prescribed cases; and
(b) prescribe, as regards any amount, a sum or a method of calculating the amount.

6–47   **46.**—(1) Any expenses which are incurred under this Act by an authorised officer of a food authority in procuring samples, and causing samples to be analysed or examined, shall be defrayed by that authority.

(2) Any expenses incurred by a county council in the enforcement and execution of any provision of this Act, or of any regulations or orders made under it, shall, if the Secretary of State so directs, be defrayed as expenses for special county purposes charged on such part of the county as may be specified in the direction.

6–48   **47.**—There shall be paid out of money provided by Parliament to the chairman of any tribunal constituted in accordance with regulations under this Act such remuneration (by way of salary or fees) and such allowances as the Ministers may with the approval of the Treasury determine.

Instruments and documents

6–49   **48.**—(1) Any power of the Ministers or the Minister to make regulations or an order under this Act includes power—

(a) to apply, with modifications and adaptations, any other enactment (including one contained in this Act) which deals with matters similar to those being dealt with by the regulations or order;
(b) to make different provision in relation to different cases or classes of case (including different provision for different areas or different classes of business); and
(c) to provide for such exceptions, limitations and conditions, and to make such supplementary, incidental, consequential or transitional provisions, as the Ministers or the Minister considers necessary or expedient.

(2) Any power of the Ministers or the Minister to make regulations or orders under this Act shall be exercisable by statutory instrument.

(3) Any statutory instrument containing—

(a) regulations under this Act; or
(b) an order under this Act other than an order under section 60(3) below.

shall be subject to annulment in pursuance of a resolution of either House of Parliament.

(4) Before making—

138

(a) any regulations under this Act, other than regulations under section 17(2) or 18(1)(c) above; or

(b) any order under Part I of this Act,

the Ministers shall consult with such organisations as appear to them to be representative of interests likely to be substantially affected by the regulations or order.

(5) Any consultation undertaken before the commencement of subsection (4) above shall be as effective, for the purposes of that subsection, as if undertaken after that commencement.

49.—(1) The following shall be in writing, namely— **6–50**

(a) all documents authorised or required by or under this Act to be given, made or issued by a food authority; and

(b) all notices and applications authorised or required by or under this Act to be given or made to, or to any officer of, such an authority.

(2) The Ministers may by regulations prescribe the form of any document to be used for any of the purposes of this Act and, if forms are so prescribed, those forms or forms to the like effect may be used in all cases to which those forms are applicable.

(3) Any document which a food authority are authorised or required by or under this Act to give, make or issue may be signed on behalf of the authority—

(a) by proper officer of the authority as respects documents relating to matters within his province; or

(b) by any officer of the authority authorised by them in writing to sign documents of the particular kind or, as the case may be, the particular document.

(4) Any document purporting to bear the signature of an officer who is expressed—

(a) to hold an office by virtue of which he is under this section empowered to sign such a document; or

(b) to be duly authorised by the food authority to sign such a document or the particular document,

shall for the purposes of this Act, and of any regulations and orders made under it, be deemed, until the contrary is proved, to have been duly given, made or issued by authority of the food authority.

(5) In this section—

"proper officer", in relation to any purpose and to any food authority or any area, means the officer appointed for that purpose by that authority or, as the case may be, for that area;

"signature" includes a facsimile of a signature by whatever process reproduced.

6–51   50.—(1) Any document which is required or authorised by or under this Act to be given to or served on any person may, in any case for which no other provision is made by this Act, be given or served either—

    (a) by delivering it to that person;

    (b) in the case of any officer of an enforcement authority, by leaving it, or sending it in a prepaid letter addressed to him, at his office;

    (c) in the case of an incorporated company or body, by delivering it to their secretary or clerk at their registered or principal office, or by sending it in a prepaid letter addressed to him at that office; or

    (d) in the case of any other person, by leaving it, or sending it in a prepaid letter addressed to him, at his usual or last known residence.

(2) Where a document is to be given to or served on the owner or the occupier of any premises and it is not practicable after reasonable inquiry to ascertain the name and address of the person to or on whom it should be given or served, or the premises are unoccupied, the document may be given or served by addressing it to the person concerned by the description of "owner" or "occupier" of the premises (naming them) and—

    (a) by delivering it to some person on the premises; or

    (b) if there is no person on the premises to whom it can be delivered, by affixing it, or a copy of it, to some conspicuous part of the premises.

Amendments of other Acts

6–52   51.—(1) Part I of the Food and Environment Protection Act 1985 (contamination of food) shall have effect, and shall be deemed always to have had effect, subject to the amendments specified in subsection (2) below.

(2) The amendments referred to in subsection (1) above are—

    (a) in subsection (1) of section 1 (power to make emergency orders), the substitution for paragraph (a) of the following paragraph—
        "(a) there exist or may exist circumstances which are likely to create a hazard to human health through human consumption of food;";

    (b) in subsection (2) of that section, the omission of the definition of "escape";

    (c) the substitution for subsection (5) of that section of the following subsection—
        "(5) An emergency order shall refer to the circumstances or suspected circumstances in consequence of which in the opinion of the designating authority making it food such as is mentioned in subsection (1)(b) above is, or may be, or may become, unsuitable for human consumption; and in this Act 'designated circumstances' means the circumstances or suspected circumstances to which an emergency order refers in pursuance of this subsection.";

    (d) in section 2(3) (powers when emergency order has been made), the substitution for the words "a designated incident" of the words "designated circumstances";

(e) in paragraph (a) of subsection (1) of section 4 (powers of officers), the substitution for the words "an escape of substances" of the words "such circumstances as are mentioned in section 1(1) above"; and

(f) in paragraphs (b) and (c) of that subsection, the substitution for the words "the designated incident" of the words "the designated circumstances".

52. In the Food Act 1984 (in this Act referred to as "the 1984 Act")—   **6–53**

(a) Part III (markets); and

(b) Part V (sugar beet and cold storage),

shall have effect subject to the amendments specified in Schedule 2 to this Act.

Supplemental

53.—(1) In this Act, unless the context otherwise requires—   **6–54**
"the 1984 Act" means the Food Act 1984;

"the 1956 Act" means the Food and Drugs (Scotland) Act 1956;

"advertisement" includes any notice, circular, label, wrapper, invoice or other document, and any public announcement made orally or by any means of producing or transmitting light or sound, and "advertise" shall be construed accordingly;

"analysis" includes microbiological assay and any technique for establishing the composition of food, and "analyse" shall be construed accordingly;

"animal" means any creature other than a bird or fish;

"article" does not include a live animal or bird, or a live fish which is not used for human consumption while it is alive;

"container" includes any basket, pail, tray, package or receptacle of any kind, whether open or closed;

"contravention", in relation to any provision, includes any failure to comply with that provision;

"cream" means that part of milk rich in fact which has been separated by skimming or otherwise;

"equipment" includes any apparatus;

"exportation" and "importation" have the same meanings as they have for the purposes of the Customs and Excise Management Act 1979 and "export" and "import" shall be construed accordingly;

"fish" includes crustaceans and mulluscs;

"functions" includes powers and duties;

"human consumption" includes use in the preparation of food for human consumption;

"knacker's yard" means any premises used in connection with the business of slaughtering, flaying or cutting up animals the flesh of which is not intended for human consumption;

"milk" includes cream and skimmed or separated milk;

"occupier", in relation to any ship or aircraft of a description specified in an order made under section 1(3) above or any vehicle, stall or place, means the master, commander or other person in charge of the ship, aircraft, vehicle, stall or place;

"officer" includes servant;

"preparation", in relation to food, includes manufacture and any form of processing or treatment, and "preparation for sale" includes packaging, and "prepare for sale" shall be construed accordingly.

"presentation", in relation to food, includes the shape, appearance and packaging of the food, the way in which the food is arranged when it is exposed for sale and the setting in which the food is displayed with a view to sale, but does not include any form of labelling or advertising, and "present" shall be construed accordingly;

"proprietor", in relation to a food business, means the person by whom that business is carried on;

"ship" includes any vessel, boat or craft, and a hovercraft within the meaning of the Hovercraft Act 1968, and "master" shall be construed accordingly.

"slaughterhouse" means a place for slaughtering animals, the flesh of which is intended for sale for human consumption, and includes any place available in connection with such a place for the confinement of animals while awaiting slaughter there or for keeping, or subjecting to any treatment or process, products of the slaughtering of animals there;

"substance" includes any natural or artificial substance or other matter, whether it is in solid or liquid form or in the form of a gas or vapour;

"treatment", in relation to any food, includes subjecting it to heat or cold.

(2) The following Table shows provisions defining or otherwise explaining expressions used in this Act (other than provisions defining or explaining an expression used only in the same section)—

authorised officer of a food authority	section 5(6)
business	section 1(3)
commercial operation	section 1(3) and (4)
contact material	section 1(3)
emergency control order	section 13(1)
emergency prohibition notice	section 12(1)
emergency prohibition order	section 12(2)
enforcement authority	section 6(1)
examination and examine	section 28(2)
food	section 1(1), (2) and (4)

food authority	section 5
food business	section 1(3)
food premises	section 1(3)
food safety requirements and related expressions	section 8(2)
food source	section 1(3)
improvement notice	section 10(1)
injury to health and injurious to health	section 7(3)
the Minister	section 4(1) and (2)
the Ministers	section 4(1)
premises	section 1(3)
prohibition order	section 11(5)
public analyst	section 27(1)
sale and related expressions	section 2
unfit for human consumption	section 8(4)

(3) Any reference in this Act to regulations or orders made under it shall be construed as a reference to regulations or orders made under this Act by the Ministers or the Minister.

(4) For the purposes of this Act, any class or description may be framed by reference to any matters or circumstances whatever, including in particular, in the case of a description of food, the brand name under which it is commonly sold.

(5) Where, apart from this subsection, any period of less than seven days which is specified in this Act would include any day which is—

(a) a Saturday, a Sunday, Christmas Day or Good Friday; or
(b) a day which is a bank holiday under the Banking and Financial Dealings Act 1971 in the part of Great Britain concerned,

that day shall be excluded from that period.

54.—(1) Subject to the provisions of this section, the provisions of this Act and of regulations and orders made under it shall bind the Crown. **6–55**

(2) No contravention by the Crown of any provision of this Act or of any regulations or order made under it shall make the Crown criminally liable; but the High Court or, in Scotland, the Court of Session may, on the application of an enforcement authority, declare unlawful any act or omission of the Crown which constitutes such a contravention.

(3) Notwithstanding anything in subsection (2) above, the provisions of this Act and of regulations and orders made under it shall apply to persons in the public service of the Crown as they apply to other persons.

(4) If the Secretary of State certifies that it appears to him requisite or expedient in the interests of national security that the powers of entry conferred by section 32 above should not be exercisable in relation to any Crown premises specified in the certificate, those powers shall not be exercisable in relation to those premises; and in

143

this subsection "Crown premises" means premises held or used by or on behalf of the Crown.

(5) Nothing in this section shall be taken as in any way affecting Her Majesty in her private capacity; and this subsection shall be construed as if section 38(3) of the Crown Proceedings Act 1947 (interpretation of references in that Act to Her Majesty in her private capacity) were contained in this Act.

6–56   55.—(1) Nothing in Part II of this Act or any regulations or order made under that Part shall apply in relation to the supply of water to any premises, whether by a water undertaker or by means of a private supply (within the meaning of Chapter II of Part II of the Water Act 1989).

(2) In the following provisions of that Act, namely—
    section 52 (duties of water undertakers with respect to water quality);

    section 53 (regulations for preserving water quality); and

    section 64 (additional powers of entry for the purposes of Chapter II),
for the words "domestic purposes", wherever they occur, there shall be substituted the words "domestic or food production purposes".

(3) In subsection (2) of section 56 of that Act (general functions of local authorities in relation to water quality), for the words "domestic purposes" there shall be substituted the words "domestic or food production purposes" and for the words "those purposes" there shall be substituted the words "domestic purposes".

(4) In subsection (1) of section 57 of that Act (remedial powers of local authorities in relation to private supplies), for the words "domestic purposes", in the first place where they occur, there shall be substituted the words "domestic or food production purposes".

(5) In subsection (1) of section 66 of that Act (interpretation etc. of Chapter II), after the definition of "consumer" there shall be inserted the following definition—

" 'food production purposes' shall be construed in accordance with subsection (1A) below;".

(6) After that subsection there shall be inserted the following subsection—

"(1A) In this Chapter references to food production purposes are references to the manufacturing, processing, preserving or marketing purposes with respect to food or drink for which water supplied to food production premises may be used; and in this subsection 'food production premises' means premises used for the purposes of a business of preparing food or drink for consumption otherwise than on the premises."

6–57   56.—(1) Nothing in Part II of this Act or any regulations or order made under that Part shall apply in relation to the supply of water to any premises, whether by a water authority (within the meaning of section 3 of the Water (Scotland) Act 1980) or by means of a private supply (within the meaning of Part VIA of that Act).

(2) In the following provisions of that Act, namely—
    section 76A (duties of water authorities with respect to water quality); and

section 76B (regulations for preserving water quality),
for the words "domestic purposes", wherever they occur, there shall be substituted the words "domestic or food production purposes".

(3) In subsection (2) of section 76F of that Act (general functions of local authorities in relation to water quality), for the words "domestic purposes" there shall be substituted the words "domestic or food production purposes" and for the words "those purposes" there shall be substituted the words "domestic purposes".

(4) In subsection (1) of section 76G of that Act (remedial powers of local authorities in relation to private supplies), for the words "domestic purposes", in the first place where they occur, there shall be substituted the words "domestic or food production purposes".

(5) In subsection (1) of section 76L of that Act (interpretation etc. of Part VIA), after the definition of "analyse" there shall be inserted the following definition—

> " 'food production purposes' shall be construed in accordance with subsection (1A) below;".

(6) After that subsection there shall be inserted the following subsection—

> "(1A) In this Part references to food production purposes are references to the manufacturing, processing, preserving or marketing purposes with respect to food or drink for which water supplied to food production premises may be used; and in this subsection 'food production premises' means premises used for the purposes of a business of preparing food or drink for consumption otherwise than on the premises."

57.—(1) This Act shall apply to the Isles of Scilly subject to such exceptions and modifications as the Ministers may by order direct.   **6–58**

(2) Her Majesty may by Order in Council direct that any of the provisions of this Act shall extend to any of the Channel Islands with such exceptions and modifications (if any) as may be specified in the Order.

58.—(1) For the purposes of this Act the territorial waters of the United Kingdom adjacent to any part of Great Britain shall be treated as situated in that part.   **6–59**

(2) An Order in Council under section 23 of the Oil and Gas (Enterprise) Act 1982 (application of civil law) may make provision for treating for the purposes of food safety legislation—

(a) any installation which is in waters to which that section applies; and
(b) any safety zone around any such installation,

as if they were situated in a specified part of the United Kingdom and for modifying such legislation in its application to such installations and safety zones.

(3) Such an Order in Council may also confer on persons of a specified description the right to require, for the purpose of facilitating the exercise of specified powers under food safety legislation—

(a) conveyance to and from any installation, including conveyance of any equipment required by them; and

(b) the provision of reasonable accommodation and means of subsistence while they are on any installation.

(4) In this section—

"food safety legislation" means this Act and any regulations and orders made under it and any corresponding provisions in Northern Ireland;

"installation" means an installation to which subsection (3) of the said section 23 applies;

"safety zone" means an area which is a safety zone by virtue of Part III of the Petroleum Act 1987; and

"specified" means specified in the Order in Council.

6–60 **59.**—(1) The enactments mentioned in Schedule 3 to this Act shall have effect subject to the amendments there specified (being minor amendments and amendments consequential on the preceding provisions of this Act).

(2) The Ministers may by order make such modifications of local Acts, and of subordinate legislation (within the meaning of the Interpretation Act 1978), as appear to them to be necessary or expedient in consequence of the provisions of this Act.

(3) The transitional provisions and savings contained in Schedule 4 to this Act shall have effect; but nothing in this subsection shall be taken as prejudicing the operation of sections 16 and 17 of the said Act of 1978 (which relate to the effect of repeals).

(4) The enactments mentioned in Schedule 5 to this Act (which include some that are spent or no longer of practical utility) are hereby repealed to the extent specified in the third column of that Schedule.

6–61 **60.**—(1) This Act may be cited as the Food Safety Act 1990.

(2) The following provisions shall come into force on the day on which this Act is passed, namely—

section 13;

section 51; and

paragraphs 12 to 15 of Schedule 2 and, so far as relating to those paragraphs, section 52.

(3) Subject to subsection (2) above, this Act shall come into force on such day as the Ministers may by order appoint, and different days may be appointed for different provisions or for different purposes.

(4) An order under subsection (3) above may make such transitional adaptations of any of the following, namely—

(a) the provisions of this Act then in force or brought into force by the order; and

146

(b) the provisions repealed by this Act whose repeal is not then in force or so brought into force,

as appear to the Ministers to be necessary or expedient in consequence of the partial operation of this Act.

(5) This Act, except—
this section;

section 51,

section 58(2) to (4), and

paragraphs 7, 29 and 30 of Schedule 3 and, so far as relating to those paragraphs, section 59(1),

does not extend to Northern Ireland.

SCHEDULES

SCHEDULE 1

PROVISIONS OF REGULATIONS UNDER SECTION 16(I)

Composition of food

1. Provision for prohibiting or regulating— **6–62**

(a) the sale, possession for sale, or offer, exposure or advertisement for sale, of any specified substance, or of any substance of any specified class, with a view to its use in the preparation of food; or
(b) the possession of any such substance for use in the preparation of food.

Fitness etc. of food

2.—(1) Provision for prohibiting— **6–63**

(a) the sale for human consumption; or
(b) the use in the manufacture of products for sale for such consumption,

of food derived from a food source which is suffering or has suffered from, or which is liable to be suffering or to have suffered from, any disease specified in the regulations.

(2) Provision for prohibiting or regulating, or for enabling enforcement authorities to prohibit or regulate—

(a) the sale for human consumption; or
(b) the offer, exposure or distribution for sale for such consumption

147

of shellfish taken from beds or other layings for the time being designated by or under the regulations.

3.—(1) Provision for regulating generally the treatment and disposal of any food—

(a) which is unfit for human consumption; or
(b) which, though not unfit for human consumption, is not intended for, or is prohibited from being sold for, such consumption.

(2) Provision for the following, namely—

(a) for the registration by enforcement authorities of premises used or proposed to be used for the purpose of sterilising meat to which sub-paragraph (1) above applies, and for prohibiting the use for that purpose of any premises which are not registered in accordance with the regulations; or
(b) for the issue by such authorities of licences in respect of the use of premises for the purpose of sterilising such meat, and for prohibiting the use for that purpose of any premises except in accordance with a licence issued under the regulations.

Processing and treatment of food

6–64   **4.** Provision for the following, namely—

(a) for the giving by persons possessing such qualifications as may be prescribed by the regulations of written opinions with respect to the use of any process or treatment in the preparation of food, and for prohibiting the use for any such purpose of any process or treatment except in accordance with an opinion given under the regulations; or
(b) for the issue by enforcement authorities of licences in respect of the use of any process or treatment in the preparation of food, and for prohibiting the use for any such purpose of any process or treatment except in accordance with a licence issued under the regulations.

Food hygiene

6–65   **5.**—(1) Provision for imposing requirements as to—

(a) the construction, maintenance, cleanliness and use of food premises, including any parts of such premises in which equipment and utensils are cleaned, or in which refuse is disposed of or stored;
(b) the provision, maintenance and cleanliness of sanitary and washing facilities in connection with such premises; and
(c) the disposal of refuse from such premises.

(2) Provision for imposing requirements as to—

(a) the maintenance and cleanliness of equipment or utensils used for the purposes of a food business; and

(b) the use, for the cleaning of equipment used for milking, of cleaning agents approved by or under the regulations.

(3) Provision for requiring persons who are or intend to become involved in food business, whether as proprietors or employees or otherwise, to undergo such food hygiene training as may be specified in the regulations.

6.—(1) Provision for imposing responsibility for compliance with any requirements imposed by virtue of paragraph 5(1) above in respect of any premises—

(a) on the occupier of the premises; and
(b) in the case of requirements of a structural character, on any owner of the premises who either—
  (i) lets them for use for a purpose to which the regulations apply; or
  (ii) permits them to be so used after notice from the authority charged with the enforcement of the regulations.

(2) Provision for conferring in relation to particular premises, subject to such limitations and safeguards as may be specified, exemptions from the operation of specified provisions which—

(a) are contained in the regulations; and
(b) are made by virtue of paragraph 5(1) above,

while there is in force a certificate of the enforcement authority to the effect that compliance with those provisions cannot reasonably be required with respect to the premises or any activities carried on in them.

Inspection etc. of food sources

7.—(1) Provision for securing the inspection of food sources by authorised officers of enforcement authorities for the purpose of ascertaining whether they—   **6–66**

(a) fail to comply with the requirements of the regulations; or
(b) are such that any food derived from them is likely to fail to comply with those requirements.

(2) Provision for enabling such an officer, if it appears to him on such an inspection that any food source falls within sub-paragraph (1)(a) or (b) above, to give notice to the person in charge of the food source that, until a time specified in the notice or until the notice is withdrawn—

(a) no commercial operations are to be carried out with respect to the food source; and
(b) the food source either is not to be removed or is not to be removed except to some place so specified.

(3) Provision for enabling such an officer, if on further investigation it appears to him, in the case of any such food source which is a live animal or bird, that there is present in the animal or bird any substance whose presence is prohibited by the regulations, to cause the animal or bird to be slaughtered.

SCHEDULE 2

AMENDMENTS OF PARTS III AND V OF 1984 ACT

Amendments of Part III

6–67   **1.** Part III of the 1984 Act (markets) shall be amended in accordance with paragraphs 2 to 11 below.

2.—(1) In subsection (1) of section 50 (establishment or acquisition of markets), for the words "The council of a district" there shall be substituted the words "A local authority" and for the words "their district", in each place where they occur, there shall be substituted the words "their area".

(2) In subsection (2) of that section, for the words "the district" there shall be substituted the words "the authority's area".

(3) For subsection (3) of that section there shall be substituted the following subsection—

> "(3) For the purposes of subsection (2), a local authority shall not be regarded as enjoying any rights, powers or privileges within another local authority's area by reason only of the fact that they maintain within their own area a market which has been established under paragraph (a) of subsection (1) or under the corresponding provision of any earlier enactment".

3. In section 51(2) (power to sell to local authority), the word "market" shall cease to have effect.

4. (1) In subsection (1) of section 53 (charges by market authority), the words "and in respect of the weighing and measuring of articles and vehicles" shall cease to have effect.

(2) For subsection (2) of that section there shall be substituted the following subsection—

> "(2) A market authority who provide—
> (a) a weighing machine for weighing cattle, sheep or swine; or
> (b) a cold air store or refrigerator for the storage and preservation of meat and other articles of food,
> may demand in respect of the weighing of such animals or, as the case may be, the use of the sotre or refrigerator such charges as they may from time to time determine."

(3) In subsection (3)(b) of that section, the words "in respect of the weighing of vehicles, or, as the case may be," shall cease to have effect.

5. For subsection (2) of section 54 (time for payment of charges) there shall be substituted the following subsection—

"(2) Charges payable in respect of the weighing of cattle, sheep or swine shall be paid in advance to an authorised market officer by the person bringing the animals to be weighed."

6. In section 56(1) (prohibited sales in market hours), for the word "district" there shall be substituted the word "area".

7. In section 57 (weighing machines and scales), subsection (1) shall cease to have effect.

8. After that section there shall be inserted the following section—

"57A.—(1) A market authority may provide a cold air store or refrigerator for the storage and preservation of meat and other articles of food.

(2) Any proposal by a market authority to provide under this section a cold air store or refrigerator within the area of another local authority requires the consent of that other authority, which shall not be unreasonably withheld.

(3) Any question whether or not such a consent is unreasonably withheld shall be referred to and determined by the Ministers.

(4) Subsections (1) to (5) of section 250 of the Local Government Act 1972 (which relate to local inquiries) shall apply for the purposes of this section as if any reference in those subsections to that Act included a reference to this section."

9. Section 58 (weighing of articles) shall cease to have effect.

10. In section 60 (market byelaws), after paragraph (c) there shall be inserted the following paragraph—

"(d)   after consulting the fire authority for the area in which the market is situated, for preventing the spread of fires in the market."

11. In section 61 (interpretation of Part III), the words from "and this Part" to the end shall cease to have effect and for the definition of "market authority" there shall be substituted the following definitions—

" 'fire authority' means an authority exercising the functions of a fire authority under the Fire Services Act 1947;
'food' has the same meaning as in the Food Safety Act 1990;
'local authority' means a district council, a London borough council or a parish or community council;
'market authority' means a local authority who maintain a market which has been established or acquired under section 50(1) or under the corresponding provisions of any earlier enactment."

151

Amendments of Part V

6–68   **12.** Part V of the 1984 Act (sugar beet and cold storage) shall be amended in accordance with paragraphs 13 to 16 below.

13. (1) In subsections (1) and (2) of section 68 (research and education), for the word "Company", wherever it occurs, there shall be substituted the words "processors of home-grown beet".

(2) After subsection (5) of that section there shall be inserted the following subsection—

> "(5A) An order under this section there shall be made by statutory instrument which shall be subject to annulment in pursuance of a resolution of either House of Parliament.".

(3) In subsection (6) of that section, for the definition of "the Company" and subsequent definitions there shall be substituted—

> " 'year' means a period of 12 months beginning with 1st April;

> and in this section and sections 69 and 69A 'home-grown beet' means sugar beet grown in Great Britain".

14. In subsection (3) of section 69 (crop price), for the words " 'home-grown beet' means sugar beet grown in Great Britain; and" there shall be substituted the words "and section 69A".

15. After that section there shall be inserted the following section—

> 69A.—(1) For the purpose of facilitating—
> (a) the making of a determination under section 69(1); or
> (b) the preparation or conduct of discussions concerning Community arrangements for or relating to the regulation of the market for sugar,
> the appropriate Minister may serve on any processor of home-grown beet a notice requiring him to furnish in writing, within such period as is specified in the notice, such information as is so specified.

> (2) Subject to subsection (3), information obtained under subsection (1) shall not be disclosed without the previous consent in writing of the person by whom the information was furnished; and a person who discloses any information so obtained in contravention of this subsection shall be liable—
> (a) on conviction on indictment, to a fine or to imprisonment for a term not exceeding two years or to both;
> (b) on summary conviction, to a fine not exceeding the statutory maximum or to imprisonment for a term not exceeding three months or to both.

> (3) Nothing in subsection (2) shall restrict the disclosure of information to any of the Ministers or the disclosure—

(a) of information obtained under subsection (1)(a)—
    (i) to a person designated to make a determination under section 69(1); or
    (ii) to a body which substantially represents the growers of home-grown beet; or
(b) of information obtained under subsection (1)(b), to the Community institution concerned.
(4) In this section "the appropriate Minister" means—
(a) in relation to England, the Minister of Agriculture, Fisheries and Food; and
(b) in relation to Scotland or Wales, the Secretary of State."

16. Section 70 (provision of cold storage) shall cease to have effect.

SCHEDULE 3

Minor and Consequential Amendments

The Public Health Act 1936 (c. 49)

1. An order made by the Secretary of State under section 6 of the Public Health
Act 1936 may constitute a united district for the purposes of any functions under
this Act which are functions of a food authority in England and Wales.   **6–69**

The London Government Act 1963 (c. 33)

2. Section 54(1) of the London Government Act 1963 (food, drugs, markets and animals) shall cease to have effect.

The Agriculture Act 1967 (c. 22)

3. In section 7(3) of the Agriculture Act 1967 (labelling of meat in relation to systems of classifying meat), the words from "and, without prejudice" to the end shall cease to have effect.

4.—(1) In subsection (2) of section 25 of that Act (interpretation of Part I), for the definition of "slaughterhouse" there shall be substituted the following definition—
    " 'slaughterhouse' has, in England and Wales, the meaning given by section 34 of the Slaughterhouses Act 1974 and, in Scotland, the meaning given by section 22 of the Slaughter of Animals (Scotland) Act 1980;".
(2) In subsection (3) of that section, for the words from "Part II" to "1955" there shall be substituted the words "section 15 of the Slaughterhouses Act 1974 or section 1 of the Slaughter of Animals (Scotland) Act 1980".

153

The Farm and Garden Chemicals Act 1967 (c. 50)

5. In section 4 of the Farm and Garden Chemicals Act 1967 (evidence of analysis of products)—

  (a) in subsection (3), for the words "section 76 of the Food Act 1984" there shall be substituted the words "section 27 of the Food Safety Act 1990"; and
  (b) in subsection (7)(c), the words from "for the reference" to "1956" shall cease to have effect.

The Trade Descriptions Act 1968 (c. 29)

6–70   **6.** In section 2(5)(a) of the Trade Descriptions Act 1968 (certain descriptions to be deemed not to be trade descriptions), for the words "the Food Act 1984, the Food and Drugs (Scotland) Act 1956" there shall be substituted the words "the Food Safety Act 1990".

7. In section 22 of that Act (admissibility of evidence in proceedings for offences under Act), in subsection (2), the paragraph beginning with the words "In this subsection" shall cease to have effect, and after that subsection there shall be inserted the following subsection—

  "(2A) In subsection (2) of this section—
    'the food and drugs laws' means the Food Safety Act 1990, the Medicines Act 1968 and the Food (Northern Ireland) Order 1989 and any instrument made thereunder;
    'the relevant provisions' means—
      (i) in relation to the said Act of 1990, section 31 and regulations made thereunder;
      (ii) in relation to the said Act of 1968, so much of Schedule 3 to that Act as is applicable to the circumstances in which the sample was procured; and
      (iii) in relation to the said Order, Articles 40 and 44,
    or any provisions replacing any of those provisions by virtue of section 17 of the said Act of 1990, paragraph 27 of Schedule 3 to the said Act of 1968 or Article 72 or 73 of the said Order."

The Medicines Act 1968 (c. 67)

6–71   **8.** In section 108 of the Medicines Act 1968 (enforcement in England and Wales)—

  (a) for the words "food and drugs authority", in each place where they occur, there shall be substituted the words "drugs authority"; and
  (b) after subsection (11) there shall be inserted the following subsection—

  "(12) In this section 'drugs authority' means—

(a) as respects each London borough, metropolitan district or non-metropolitan county, the council of that borough, district or county; and

(b) as respects the City of London (including the Temples), the Common Council of that City."

9. In section 109 of that Act (enforcement in Scotland)—

(a) paragraph (c) of subsection (2) shall cease to have effect; and

(b) after that subsection there shall be inserted the following subsection—

"(2A) Subsection (12) of section 108 of this Act shall have effect in relation to Scotland as if for paragraphs (a) and (b) there were substituted the words "an islands or district council".

10. After section 115 of that Act there shall be inserted the following section—

"115A. A drugs authority or the council of a non-metropolitan district may provide facilities for microbiological examinations of drugs."

11. In section 132(1) of that Act (interpretation), the definition of "food and drugs authority" shall cease to have effect and after the definition of "doctor" there shall be inserted the following definition—

" 'drugs authority' has the meaning assigned to it by section 108(12) of this Act;".

12. In paragraph 1(2) of Schedule 3 to that Act (sampling) for the words from "in relation to England and Wales" to "Food and Drugs (Scotland) Act 1956" there shall be substituted the words "except in relation to Northern Ireland, has the meaning assigned to it by section 27 of the Food Safety Act 1990".

The Transport Act 1968 (c. 73)

13. In Schedule 16 to the Transport Act 1968 (supplementary and consequential provisions), in paragraph 7(2), paragraphs (d) and (e) shall cease to have effect.

The Tribunals and Inquiries Act 1971 (c. 62)

14. (1) In Schedule 1 to the Tribunals and Inquiries Act 1971 (tribunals under supervision of Council on Tribunals), paragraph 15 shall cease to have effect and after paragraph 6B there shall be inserted the following paragraph:

6–72

"Food	6C. Tribunals constituted in accordance with regulations under Part II of the Food Safety Act 1990."

155

(2) In that Schedule, paragraph 40 shall cease to have effect and after paragraph 36 there shall be inserted the following paragraph—

"Food	36A. Tribunals constituted in accordance with regulations under Part II of the Food Safety Act 1990 being tribunals appointed for Scotland."

The Agriculture (Miscellaneous Provisions) Act 1972 (c. 62)

15.—(1) In subsection (1) of section 4 of the Agriculture (Miscellaneous Provisions) Act 1972 (furnishing by milk marketing boards of information derived from tests of milk)—

    (a) for the words "appropriate authority" there shall be substituted the words "enforcement authority"; and

    (b) for the words from "Milk and Dairies Regulations" to "1956" there shall be substituted the words "regulations relating, to milk, dairies or dairy farms which were made under, or have effect as if made under, section 16 of the Food Safety Act 1990."

(2) In subsection (2) of that section, for the definition of "appropriate authority" there shall be substituted the following definition—

      " 'enforcement authority' has the same meaning as in the Food Safety Act 1990;".

(3) Subsection (3) of that section shall cease to have effect.

The Poisons Act 1972 (c. 66)

6–73   **16.** In section 8(4)(a) of the Poisons Act 1972 (evidence of analysis in proceedings under Act) for the words "section 76 of the Food Act 1984, or section 27 of the Food and Drugs (Scotland) Act 1956" there shall be substituted the words "section 27 of the Food Safety Act 1990".

The Local Government Act 1972 (c. 70)

17. In section 259(3) of the Local Government Act 1972 (compensation for loss of office)—

    (a) in paragraph (b), for the words "food and drugs authority, within the meaning of the Food Act 1984" there shall be substituted the words "food authority within the meaning of the Food Safety Act 1990";

    (b) in paragraph (c), for sub-paragraphs (i) and (ii) there shall be substituted the words "which are incorporated or reproduced in the Slaughterhouses Act 1974 or the Food Safety Act 1990"; and

    (c) the words "section 129(1) of the Food and Drugs Act 1955" shall cease to have effect.

The Slaughterhouses Act 1974 (c. 3)

18. In the following provisions of the Slaughterhouses Act 1974, namely—

    (a) section 2(2)(a) (requirements to be complied with in relation to slaughter-house licences);

    (b) section 4(2)(a) (requirements to be complied with in relation to knacker's yard licences);

    (c) section 12(2) (regulations with respect to slaughterhouses and knackers' yards to prevail over byelaws); and

    (d) section 16(3) (regulations with respect to public slaughterhouses to prevail over byelaws),

for the words "section 13 of the Food Act 1984" there shall be substituted the words "section 16 of the Food Safety Act 1990".

The Licensing (Scotland) Act 1976 (c. 66)

19. In section 23(4) of the Licensing (Scotland) Act 1976 (application for new licence), for the words "section 13 of the Food and Drugs (Scotland) Act 1956" there shall be substituted "section 16 of the Food Safety Act 1990". **6–74**

The Weights and Measures &c. Act 1976 (c. 77)

20.—(1) In subsection (1) of section 12 of the Weights and Measures &c. Act 1976 (shortages of food and other goods), for paragraphs (a) and (b) there shall be substituted the following paragraph—

    "(a)   section 16 of the Food Safety Act 1990 ('the 1990 Act');".

(2) In subsection (9) of that section—

    (a) for paragraph (a) there shall be substituted the following paragraph—

        "(a)   where it was imposed under the 1990 Act—

            (i) the Minister of Agriculture, Fisheries and Food and the Secretary of State acting jointly in so far as it was imposed in relation to England and Wales; and

            (ii) the Secretary of State in so far as it was imposed in relation to Scotland;";and

    (b) in paragraph (c), the words "the 1956 Act or" shall cease to have effect.

21. In Schedule 6 to that Act (temporary requirements imposed by emergency orders), for paragraphs 2 and 3 there shall be substituted the following paragraph—

"Food Safety Act 1990 (c. 16)

2. (1) This paragraph applies where the relevant requirement took effect under or by virtue of the Food Safety Act 1990.

(2) The following provisions of that Act—

157

(a) Part I (preliminary);
(b) Part III (administration and enforcement); and
(c) sections 40 to 50 (default powers and other supplemental provisions),

shall apply as if the substituted requirement were imposed by regulations under section 16 of that Act."

The Hydrocarbon Oil Duties Act 1979 (c. 5)

6–75 **22.** In Schedule 5 to the Hydrocarbon Oil Duties Act 1979 (sampling) in paragraph 5(d) for the words "section 76 of the Food Act 1984, section 27 of the Food and Drugs (Scotland) Act 1956" there shall be substituted the words "section 27 of the Food Safety Act 1990".

The Slaughter of Animals (Scotland) Act 1980 (c. 13)

23. In section 19(2) of the Slaughter of Animals (Scotland) Act 1980 (enforcement) for the words "section 13 of the Food and Drugs (Scotland) Act 1956" there shall be substituted the words "section 16 of the Food Safety Act 1990" and for the words "section 36 of the said Act of 1956" there shall be substituted the words "section 32 of the said Act of 1990".

24. In section 22 of that Act (interpretation)—

(a) for the definition of "knacker's yard" there shall be substituted the following definition—
" 'knacker's yard' means any premises used in connection with the business of slaughtering, flaying or cutting up animals the flesh of which is not intended for human consumption; and 'knacker' means a person whose business it is to carry out such slaughtering, flaying or cutting up"; and
(b) for the definition of "slaughterhouse" there shall be substituted the following definition—
" 'slaughterhouse' means a place for slaughtering animals, the flesh of which is intended for human consumption, and includes any place available in connection with such a place for the confinement of animals while awaiting slaughter there or keeping, or subjecting to any treatment or process, products of the slaughtering of animals there; and 'slaughterman' means a person whose business it is to carry out such slaughtering".

The Civic Government (Scotland) Act 1982 (c. 45)

25. In section 39 of the Civic Government (Scotland) Act 1982 (street traders' licences)—

(a) in subsection (3)(b), for the words "section 7 of the Milk and Dairies (Scotland) Act 1914" there shall be substituted the words "regulations made under section 19 of the Food Safety Act 1990"; and

(b) in subsection (4)—

    (i) for the words "regulations made under sections 13 and 56 of the Food and Drugs (Scotland) Act 1956", there shall be substituted the words "section 1(3) of the Food Safety Act 1990";

    (ii) for the words "islands or district council" there shall be substituted the words "food authority (for the purposes of section 5 of the Food Safety Act 1990)"; and

    (iii) for the words "sections 13 and 56 of the Food and Drugs (Scotland) Act 1956", there shall be substituted the words "section 16 of the Food Safety Act 1990".

The Public Health (Control of Disease) Act 1984 (c. 22)

26. In section 3(2) of the Public Health (Control of Disease) Act 1984 (jurisdiction and powers of port health authority), for paragraph (a) there shall be substituted the following paragraph—   **6–76**

    "(a) of a food authority under the Food Safety Act 1990;".

27. In section 7(3) of that Act (London port health authority), for paragraph (d) there shall be substituted the following paragraph—

    "(d) of a food authority under any provision of the Food Safety Act 1990."

28. (1) In subsection (1) of section 20 of that Act (stopping of work to prevent spread of disease), in paragraph (b) for the words "subsection (1) of section 28 of the Food Act 1984" there shall be substituted "subsection (1A) below".

(2) After that subsection there shall be inserted the following subsection—

    "(1A) The diseases to which this subsection applies are—
    (a) enteric fever (including typhoid and paratyphoid fevers);
    (b) dysentry;
    (c) diphtheria;
    (d) scarlet fever;
    (e) acute inflammation of the throat;
    (f) gastro-enteritis; and
    (g) undulant fever."

The Food and Environment Protection Act 1985 (c. 48)

29. In section 24(1) of the Food and Environment Protection Act 1985 (interpretation)—

    (a) in the definition of "designated incident", for the words "designated incident" there shall be substituted the words "designated circumstances";

    (b) the definition of "escape" shall cease to have effect; and

    (c) for the definition of "food' there shall be substituted—

    " 'food' has the same meaning as in the Food Safety Act 1990."

159

30. In section 25 of that Act (Northern Ireland) after subsection (4) there shall be inserted the following subsection—

> "(4A) Section 24(1) above shall have effect in relation to Northern Ireland as if for the definition of 'food' there were substituted the following definition—
> ' "food" has the meaning assigned to it by Article 2(2) of the Food (Northern Ireland) Order 1989, except that it includes water which is bottled or is an ingredient of food;'."

The Local Government Act 1985 (c. 51)

6–77   **31.** In paragraph 15 of Schedule 8 to the Local Government Act 1985 (trading standards and related functions)—

(a) sub-paragraph (2) shall cease to have effect; and
(b) at the end of sub-paragraph (6) there shall be added the words "or section 5(1) of the Food Safety Act 1990".

The Weights and Measures Act 1985 (c. 72)

32. In section 38 of the Weights and Measures Act 1985 (special powers of inspectors), subsection (4) (exclusion for milk) shall cease to have effect.

33. In section 93 of that Act (powers under other Acts with respect to marking of food) for the words "Food Act 1984" there shall be substituted the words "Food Safety Act 1990".

34. In section 94(1) of that Act (interpretation), in the definition of "drugs" and "food" for the words "Food Act 1984, or, in Scotland, the Food and Drugs (Scotland) Act 1956" there shall be substituted the words "Food Safety Act 1990".

The Agriculture Act 1986 (c. 49)

35. In section 1(6) of the Agriculture Act 1986 (provision of agricultural goods and services), in the definition of "food", for the words "Food Act 1984" there shall be substituted "Food Safety Act 1990".

The National Health Service (Amendment) Act 1986 (c. 66)

6–78   **36.**—(1) In subsection (2) of section 1 of the National Health Service (Amendment) Act 1986 (application of food legislation to health authorities and health service premises)—

(a) for the words "appropriate authority" there shall be substituted the word "Ministers"; and
(b) for the word "authority" there shall be substituted the word "Ministers".

(2) For subsection (7) of that section there shall be substituted—

"(7) In this section—

'the Ministers' has the same meaning as in the Food Safety Act 1990;

'the food legislation' means the Food Safety Act 1990 and any regulations or orders made (or having effect as if made) under it;

'health authority'—

(a) as respects England and Wales, has the meaning assigned to it by section 128 of the 1977 Act; and

(b) as respects Scotland, means a Health Board constituted under section 2 of the 1978 Act, the Common Services Agency constituted under section 10 of that Act or a State Hospital Management Committee constituted under section 91 of the Mental Health (Scotland) Act 1984."

The Consumer Protection Act 1987 (c. 43)

37. In section 19(1) of the Consumer Protection Act 1987 (interpretation of Part II), in the definition of "food" for the words "Food Act 1984" there shall be substituted "Food Safety Act 1990".

The Road Traffic Offenders Act 1988 (c. 53)

38. In section 16(7) of the Road Traffic Offenders Act 1988 (meaning of "authorised analyst" in relation to proceedings under Act), for the words "section 76 of the Food Act 1984, or section 27 of the Food and Drugs (Scotland) Act 1956" there shall be substituted the words "section 27 of the Food Safety Act 1990".

SCHEDULE 4

TRANSITIONAL PROVISIONS AND SAVINGS

Ships and aircraft

1. In relation to any time before the commencement of the first order under section 1(3) of this Act—   **6–79**

(a) any ship which is a home-going ship within the meaning of section 132 of the 1984 Act or section 58 of the 1956 Act (interpretation) shall be regarded as premises for the purposes of this Act; and

(b) the powers of entry conferred by section 32 of this Act shall include the right to enter any ship or aircraft for the purpose of ascertaining whether there is in the ship or aircraft any food imported as part of the cargo in contravention of the provisions of regulations made under Part II of this Act;

and in this Act as it applies by virtue of this paragraph "occupier", in relation to any ship or aircraft, means the master, commander or other person in charge of the ship or aircraft.

161

Regulations under the 1984 Act

2. (1) In so far as any existing regulations made, or having effect as if made, under any provision of the 1984 Act specified in the first column of Table A below have effect in relation to England and Wales, they shall have effect, after the commencement of the relevant appeal, as if made under the provisions of this Act specified in relation to that provision in the second column of that Table, or such of those provisions as are applicable.

(2) In this paragraph and paragraphs 3 and 4 below "existing regulations" means—

> (a) any regulations made, or having effect as if made, under a provision repealed by this Act; and
> (b) any orders having effect as if made under such regulations,

which are in force immediately before the coming into force of that repeal; and references to the commencement of the relevant repeal shall be construed accordingly.

TABLE A

6–80

Provision of the 1984 Act	*Provision of this Act*
section 4 (composition etc. of food)	sections 16(1)(a), (c) and (f) and (3) and 17(1)
section 7 (describing food)	section 16(1)(e)
section 13 (food hygiene)	section 16(1)(b), (c), (d) and (f), (2) and (3)
section 33 (milk and dairies)	section 16(1)(b), (c), (d) and (f), (2) and (3)
section 34 (registration), so far as relating to dairies or dairy farms	section 19
section 38 (milk: special designations)	section 18(2)
section 73(2) (qualification of officers)	section 5(6)
section 76(2) (public analysts)	section 27(2)
section 79(5) (form of certificate)	section 49(2)
section 119 (Community provisions)	section 17(2)

Regulations under the 1956 Act

3. Any existing regulations made, or having effect as if made, under any provision of the 1956 Act specified in the first column of Table B below shall have effect, after the commencement of the relevant repeal, as if made under the provisions of this Act specified in relation to that provision in the second column of that Table, or such of those provisions as are applicable.

TABLE B

Provision of the 1956 Act	Provision of this Act
section 4 (composition etc. of food)	sections 16(1)(a), (c) and (f) and (3) and 17(1)
section 7 (describing food)	section 16(1)(e)
section 13 (food hygiene)	sections 5(6) and 16(1)(b), (c), (d) and (f), (2) and (3)
section 16(2) (regulations as to milk)	section 18(2)
section 27(2) (public analysts)	section 27(2)
section 29(3) (form of certificate)	section 49(2)
section 56A (Community provisions)	section 17(2)

OTHER REGULATIONS

4. In so far as any existing regulations made under section 1 of the Importation of **6–81** Milk Act 1983 have effect in relation to Great Britain, they shall have effect, after the commencement of the relevant repeal, as if made under section 18(1)(b) of this Act.

ORDERS WITH RESPECT TO MILK IN SCOTLAND

5.—(1) Any existing order made under section 12(2) of the Milk and Dairies (Scotland) Act 1914 (orders with respect to milk) shall have effect, after the commencement of the relevant repeal, as if it were regulations made under section 16(1)(b), (d) and (f) and (2) of this Act.

(2) Any existing order made under section 3 of the Milk and Dairies (Amendment) Act 1922 (sale of milk under special designations) shall have effect, after the commencement of the relevant repeal, as if it were regulations made under section 18(2) of this Act.

(3) In this paragraph "existing order" means any order made under a provision repealed by this Act which is in force immediately before the coming into force of that repeal; and references to the commencement of the relevant repeal shall be construed accordingly.

DISQUALIFICATION ORDERS

6. The repeal by this Act of section 14 of the 1984 Act (court's power to disqualify caterers) shall not have effect as respects any order made, or having effect as if made, under that section which is in force immediately before the commencement of that repeal.

FOOD HYGIENE BYELAWS

7.—(1) The repeal by this Act of section 15 of the 1984 Act (byelaws as to food) shall not have effect as respects any byelaws made, or having effect as if made, under that section which are in force immediately before the commencement of that repeal.

(2) In so far as any such byelaws conflict with any regulations made, or having effect as if made, under Part II of this Act, the regulations shall prevail.

CLOSURE ORDERS

8. The repeal by this Act of section 21 of the 1984 Act or section 1 of the Control of Food Premises (Scotland) Act 1977 (closure orders) shall not have effect as respects any order made, or having effect as if made, under that section which is in force immediately before the commencement of that repeal.

SCHEDULE 5

REPEALS

	Chapter	Short title	Extent of repeal
6–82	1914 c. 46.	The Milk and Dairies (Scotland) Act 1914.	The whole Act.
	1922 c. 54.	The Milk and Dairies (Amendment) Act 1922.	The whole Act.
	1934 c. 51.	The Milk Act 1934.	The whole Act.
	1949 c. 34.	The Milk (Special Designations) Act 1949.	The whole Act.
	1956 c. 30.	The Food and Drugs (Scotland) Act 1956.	The whole Act.
	1963 c. 33.	The London Government Act 1963.	Section 54(1).

1967 c. 22.	The Agriculture Act 1967.	In section 7(3), the words from "and, without prejudice" to the end.
1967 c. 50.	The Farm and Garden Chemicals Act 1967.	In section 4(7)(c), the words from "for the reference" to "1956".
1968 c. 29.	The Trade Descriptions Act 1968.	In section 22(2), the paragraph beginning with the words "In this subsection".
1968 c. 67.	The Medicines Act 1968.	In section 132(1), the definition of "food and drugs authority". In Schedule 5, paragraph 17.
1968 c. 73.	The Transport Act 1968.	In Schedule 16, in paragraph 7(2), paragraphs (d) and (e).
1971 c. 62.	The Tribunals and Inquiries Act 1971.	In Schedule 1, paragraphs 15 and 40.
1972 c. 66.	The Agriculture (Miscellaneous Provisions) Act 1972.	Section 4(3).
1972 c. 68.	The European Communities Act 1972.	In Schedule 4, paragraph 3(2)(c).
1976 c. 77.	The Weights and Measures &c. Act 1976.	In section 12(9)(c), the words "the 1956 Act or".
1977 c. 28.	The Control of Food Premises (Scotland) Act 1977.	The whole Act.
1983 c. 37.	The Importations of Milk Act 1983.	The whole Act.

165

1984 c. 30.	The Food Act 1984.	Parts I and II. In section 51(2), the word "market". In section 53, in subsection (1) the words "and in respect of the weighing and measuring of articles and vehicles", and in subsection (3)(b) the words "in respect of the weighing of vehicles, or as the case may be," Section 57(1). Section 58. In section 61, the words from "and this Part" to the end. Part IV. Sections 70 to 92. In section 93, in subsection (2), paragraphs (b) to (d) and, in subsection (3), paragraphs (a) to (e) and (h) to (l). In section 94, subsection (1) except as regards offences under Part III of the Act, and subsection (2). In section 95, subsections (2) to (8). Sections 96 to 109. Sections 111 to 120. In section 121, subsections (2) and (3). Sections 122 to 131. In section 132, subsection (1) except the words "In this Act, unless the context otherwise requires" and the definitions of "animal" and "the Minister". Sections 133 and 134. In section 136, in subsection (2), paragraphs (b) and (c). Schedules 1 to 11.
1985 c. 48.	The Food and Environment Protection Act 1985.	In section 1(2), the definition of "escape". In section 24(1), the definition of "escape".

| 1985 c. 51. | The Local Government Act 1985. | In Schedule 8, paragraph 15(2). |
| 1985 c. 72. | The Weights and Measures Act 1985. | Section 38(4). |

Code of Practice No. 6

(The rest of the Code has not been reproduced here)

SCHEDULE OF HYGIENE AND PROCESSING REGULATIONS COVERED BY THE CODE IN RESPECT OF:

ENGLAND AND WALES

Public Health (Shell-Fish) Regulations 1934   **7–01**
Milk and Dairies (General) Regulations 1959
Ice-cream (Heat Treatment, etc) Regulations 1959
Food Hygiene (Docks, Carriers, etc) Regulations 1960
Liquid Egg (Pasteurisation) Regulations 1963
Meat (Treatment) Regulations 1964
Food Hygiene (Markets, Stalls and Delivery Vehicles) Regulations 1966 (as amended in 1990)
Food (Control of Irradiation) Regulations 1967
Food Hygiene (General) Regulations 1970 (as amended in 1990)
Poultry Meat (Hygiene) Regulations 1976
Drinking Milk Regulations 1976
Slaughterhouses (Hygiene) Regulations 1977 (as amended in 1987)
Meat (Staining and Sterilising) Regulations 1982
Milk-Based Drinks (Hygiene and Health Treatment) Regulations 1983
Milk and Dairies (Heat Treatment of Cream) Regulations 1983
Fresh Meat Export (Hygiene and Inspection) Regulations 1987
Milk and Dairies (Semi-Skimmed and Skimmed Milk) (Heat Treatment and Labelling) Regulations 1988
Bovine Offal (Prohibition) Regulations 1989
Milk (Special Designations) Regulations 1989
Ungraded Eggs (Hygiene) Regulations 1990

SCOTLAND

Ice-cream (Scotland) Regulations 1948
Food Hygiene (Scotland) Regulations 1959 (as amended and consolidated in 1991)
Liquid Egg (Pasteurisation) (Scotland) Regulations 1963
Food (Control of Irradiation) (Scotland) Regulations 1967
Poultry Meat (Hygiene) (Scotland) Regulations 1976 (as amended in 1979 and 1981)
Drinking Milk (Scotland) Regulations 1976
Slaughterhouse Hygiene (Scotland) Regulations 1978 (as amended in 1987)

Meat and Poultry Meat (Staining and Sterilisation) (Scotland) Regulations 1983
Cream (Heat Treatment) (Scotland) Regulations 1983 (as amended in 1985, 1986 and 1990)
Milk-Based Drinks (Scotland) Regulations 1983 (as amended in 1986)
Fresh Meat Export (Hygiene and Inspection) (Scotland) Regulations 1987
Food (Meat Inspection) (Scotland) Regulations 1988
Milk and Dairies (Semi-Skimmed and Skimmed Milk) Heat Treatment (Scotland) Regulations 1988
Milk (Special Designations) (Scotland) Order 1988
Bovine Offal (Prohibition) (Scotland) Regulations 1990
Ungraded Eggs (Hygiene) (Scotland) 1990
Milk and Dairies (Scotland) Regulations 1990

Index

[All references are to paragraph numbers]